BWD
ANN

D0351577

Finishing Magic

★ ★ ★ ★

Dressing Up Naked Furniture with Woodgraining Techniques

BILL RUSSELL

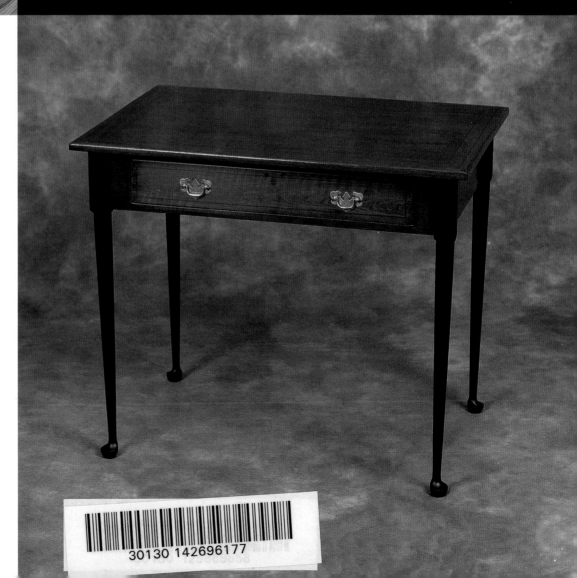

POPULAR WOODWORKING BOOKS

CINCINNATI, OHIO
www.popularwoodworking.com

30130 142696177

READ THIS IMPORTANT SAFETY NOTICE

To prevent accidents, keep safety in mind while you work. Use the safety guards installed on power equipment; they are for your protection. When working on power equipment, keep fingers away from saw blades, wear safety goggles to prevent injuries from flying wood chips and sawdust, wear headphones to protect your hearing, and consider installing a dust vacuum to reduce the amount of airborne sawdust in your woodshop. Don't wear loose clothing, such as neckties or shirts with loose sleeves, or jewelry, such as rings, necklaces or bracelets, when working on power equipment. Tie back long hair to prevent it from getting caught in your equipment. People who are sensitive to certain chemicals should check the chemical content of any product before using it. The author and editors who compiled this book have tried to make the contents as accurate and correct as possible. Plans, illustrations, photographs and text have been carefully checked. All instructions, plans and projects should be carefully read, studied and understood before beginning construction. Due to the variability of local conditions, construction materials, skill levels, etc., neither the author nor Popular Woodworking Books assumes any responsibility for any accidents, injuries, damages or other losses incurred resulting from the material presented in this book.

METRIC CONVERSION CHART

TO CONVERT	TO	MULTIPLY BY
Inches	Centimeters	2.54
Centimeters	Inches	0.4
Feet	Centimeters	30.5
Centimeters	Feet	0.03
Yards	Meters	0.9
Meters	Yards	1.1
Sq. Inches	Sq. Centimeters	6.45
Sq. Centimeters	Sq. Inches	0.16
Sq. Feet	Sq. Meters	0.09
Sq. Meters	Sq. Feet	10.8
Sq. Yards	Sq. Meters	0.8
Sq. Meters	Sq. Yards	1.2
Pounds	Kilograms	0.45
Kilograms	Pounds	2.2
Ounces	Grams	28.4
Grams	Ounces	0.04

Finishing Magic. Copyright © 2001 by Bill Russell. Manufactured in China. All rights reserved. No part of this book may be reproduced in any form or by any electronic or mechanical means including information storage and retrieval systems without permission in writing from the publisher, except by a reviewer, who may quote brief passages in a review. Published by Popular Woodworking Books, an imprint of F&W Publications, Inc., 1507 Dana Avenue, Cincinnati, Ohio, 45207. First edition.

Visit our Web site at www.popularwoodworking.com for information and resources for woodworkers.

Other fine Popular Woodworking Books are available from your local bookstore or direct from the publisher.

05   04   03   02   01   5   4   3   2   1

Library of Congress Cataloging-in-Publication Data

Russell, Bill, 1946–
    Finishing magic / by Bill Russell.
        p. cm.
    Includes index.
    ISBN 1-55870-562-7 (alk. paper)
    1. Furniture painting. 2. Finishes and finishing. I. Title.

TT199.4 .R88 2001
684.1'043--dc21   00-068448

Edited by Michael Berger and Jennifer Churchill
Cover Designed by Lou Beckmeyer
Interior Designed by Brian Roeth
Interior Production by Ben Rucker
Production Coordinated by Sara Dumford

ESSEX COUNTY COUNCIL
LIBRARIES

12586985 H

About the author

Bill Russell was born, raised and educated in Ohio, completing degrees in art at Kent State University and Miami University in Oxford, Ohio. He has taught art to students of all ages and degrees of sophistication from kindergarten to the college postgraduate level. He currently teaches drawing at Philadelphia University.

Bill worked for a number of years in antique restoration and refinishing, and it was his dual interest in painting and furniture that led to his interest in painted finishes. As a result, in 1986 he founded the Bill Russell Studio, which specializes in custom decorative painting for furniture. Besides selling his original work at his own and other galleries, Bill has completed numerous commissions for both public and private clients.

In addition to decorative painting, Bill has exhibited artwork in a variety of mediums at museums and galleries throughout the United States.

His previous book, *Decorative Furniture Finishes With Vinegar Paint*, was published by North Light Books.

Bill and his wife, Mary Galgon, have two sons, Miles and Ian. They reside in the Center City district of Philadelphia.

Acknowledgements

First I would like to thank my wife, Mary, and sons, Miles and Ian, for accepting, with good cheer, the time I have spent in the studio and in front of the computer over the several months I have been working on this book.

I would also like to thank the staff at Popular Woodworking Books and especially my editor, Mike Berger, for the invaluable help, motivation and expertise they have provided in bringing the book to fruition.

For their generosity in sharing information on various aspects of the graining art, I would like to thank Pierre Finkelstein and Allen, Ina and Robert Marx, whose books, teaching and work have been highly inspirational and informative.

I would also like to thank Scott Slezak for his good cheer and encouragement throughout the project, and Andre Fulton for his assistance with preparing the furniture.

For their help in supplying the furniture for the projects, I would like to thank the owners of London Grove Furniture.

I am especially grateful to decorative painter and longtime friend Conlon Keator for his continuing camaraderie and technical assistance. He also was kind enough to allow me to use his photo of "Big Red."

A number of craftsmen helped me in my search for particular wood samples and with technical help in the area of wood identification. Thanks to Bob Ingram, Alan Lorn, Mike Baier and especially to Jeff Weiss, Shelley Cravetz and Jack Larimore for allowing me to use photos of their work.

I owe a debt of gratitude to my photographer and friend Greg Benson, who took the beauty shots of the finished projects. His assistance and valuable advice are in evidence throughout the book.

Finally I would like to thank my clients, who have been so supportive of my work for the last 15 years as I have explored the various aspects of decorative painting.

DEDICATION

To my mother, Mary Adams Russell, and father, Richard G. Russell, whose high values and dedication to their family have provided the foundation for whatever success I have achieved.

TABLE OF *contents*

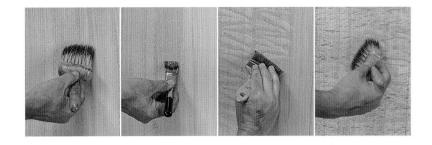

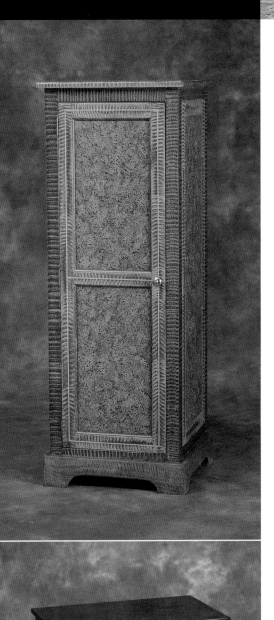

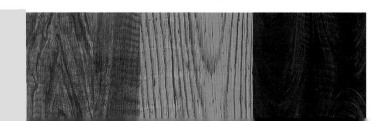

woodgraining: *an overview*

The process of painting a surface to imitate exotic or rare woods has a long history that goes all the way back to the early Egyptian times. Artists have either attempted to accurately depict the color and pattern of wood to fool the observer into thinking it was the real thing, or they have taken a more fanciful route, drawing on the general characteristics of certain woods but interpreting these characteristics in a broad or fanciful fashion. While both approaches to woodgraining offer a wide range of aesthetic possibilities, this book shows you how to reproduce the look of expensive or exotic woodgrain so convincingly that the general observer will indeed believe it is genuine.

WHY WOODGRAINING?

The reasons for woodgraining (also called grain painting) are many, but a look at one historical example can tell you much about the motivations for its use. One occasionally finds old exterior oak doors that have been grain painted to look like oak. While this may seem perverse, upon closer consideration it can actually tell you something of the confluence of the aesthetic and the practical. Oak is a very strong, durable wood of considerable beauty. If you are a homeowner, these are just the qualities you would want in your doors. But oak discolors when exposed to weather and, like most wood, requires protection from the elements. Early varnishes did not hold up well in exterior applications, so paint was more often used to protect exterior surfaces.

So the homeowner in days gone by was presented with a dilemma. His house had a beautiful, strong, expensive oak door (obviously to impress the neighbors), but in order to protect the door, he needed to paint over it. And if he painted over it, how could his neighbors tell he had an expensive door to begin with? The solution: Paint the door to protect it, but grain it as oak to reestablish the visual qualities of beauty, strength and value.

This interesting example shows a complex relationship of practical, social and aesthetic motivation for grain painting. Some others reasons for grain painting throughout history have been:

- to provide visual delight through color and pattern
- to convince the viewer that a rare, more interesting or more expensive wood has been used
- to disguise a nonwood material as wood
- to match existing wood color and pattern for repair, replacement or addition to a set
- for the sheer fun or irony of the deception

Woodgraining can be done on metal or other nonwood surfaces for a whimsical or ironic result, as this grained truck by California decorative artist Conlon Keator so effectively demonstrates.

The annual rings of this log reveal the age of the tree and will provide the characteristic pattern of heart and straight grains when the tree is cut into lumber.

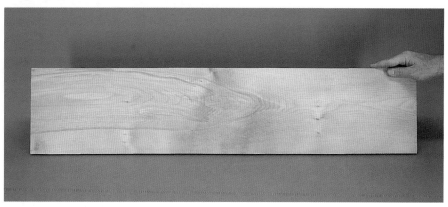

This ash board shows the typical V-shape heart grain in the center and the straight-grain lines at the sides of the board.

WHY WOOD LOOKS LIKE WOOD

You need to be aware of certain basic qualities of wood in order to paint it effectively. When a tree is cut down, the annual growth rings of the wood are exposed. During the tree's life, one ring is added each year and, by counting the rings, one can determine the age of the tree. Typically there is an alternation of darker and lighter colors to the rings. As the logs are cut lengthwise into boards, these rings show up as elongated linear patterns usually forming a series of Vs bordered by rows of straighter lines. Depending on where in the log the board comes from and the age of the tree, the board may show mostly Vs, known as heart grain, mostly straight grain or a combination of both.

While there are obvious differences in grain color and pattern from species to species, some other factors that affect the look of cut lumber are:

- the climatic and soil conditions under which the tree grew
- the age of the tree when harvested
- whether the log was straight or curved
- where from within the tree the lumber was cut
- the technique used to turn the log into boards or veneer
- deformations caused by insect and bacteria attack and other types of stress

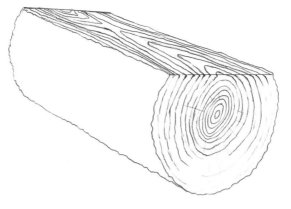

This drawing shows a log with the heart and straight grain revealed with a section removed. Curvature and change in diameter of the log create the change in direction of the Vs.

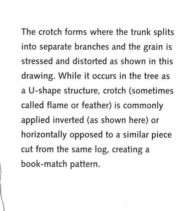

The crotch forms where the trunk splits into separate branches and the grain is stressed and distorted as shown in this drawing. While it occurs in the tree as a U-shape structure, crotch (sometimes called flame or feather) is commonly applied inverted (as shown here) or horizontally opposed to a similar piece cut from the same log, creating a book-match pattern.

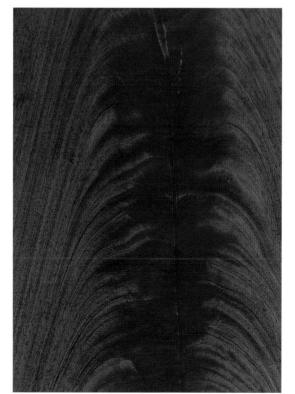

This piece of mahogany veneer, cut from the "crotch" of a tree, exhibits a distinctive pattern, which is highly prized and has been used for centuries in the finest furniture.

SPECIAL WOOD APPEARANCES

Besides being cut into boards for structural use, logs are also cut into very thin layers for use as veneer. In furniture making, veneer (which in some cases is only a fraction of an inch thick) is applied over less valuable structural woods. Depending on how the veneer is cut from the log, it may have a grain pattern similar to or very different from lumber cut from the same species. Veneer pieces are often applied to create patterns by varying the direction of the grain.

Another special and expensive appearance is burl (sometimes referred to as burr veneer), which is cut from lumpy growths found on certain trees. Burl patterns aren't linear as is typical of most woods but are formed of concentric or splotchy arrangements of knots and twisted grain. Since these growths are usually small and unstable (due to their unusual grain pattern), they are generally used as veneer, often as part of an inlay design.

Many things besides the species type, growth and harvesting process can affect the visual qualities of wood. It may be stained, oxidized, bleached, fumed and polished. It may decay, absorb oils or have various coatings applied to it. Whether these things occur naturally or are done purposely by humans, they can significantly alter the appearance of a wooden surface.

This drawing shows the two common ways lumber is cut from logs. The bottom of the log shows how lumber is plain-sawn (or flat-sawn) resulting in the heart-grain pattern. The top right section shows how lumber is quartersawn (or radially sawn) to create straight-grain lumber.

Insect and other types of infestation cause unusual grain patterns as this red maple chest by furniture artists Jeff Weiss and Shelley Cravetz shows. Commonly known as ghost maple, this pattern results from moth larvae boring through the log. The subsequent fungal attack creates the dark streaks in the lumber, which these artists exploited with striking results.

PHOTO BY PAT SIMONE

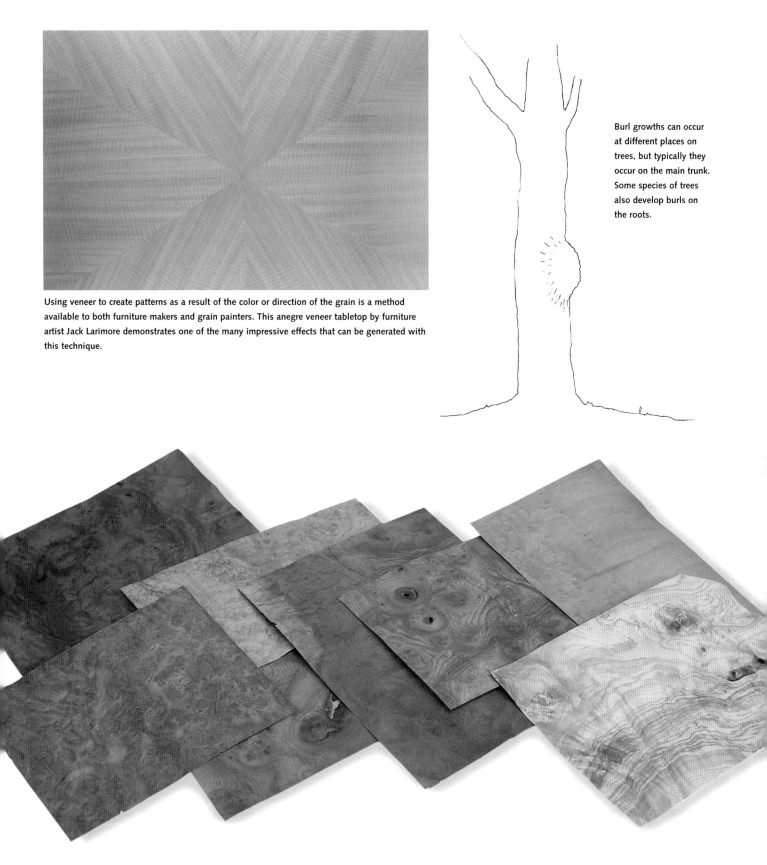

Using veneer to create patterns as a result of the color or direction of the grain is a method available to both furniture makers and grain painters. This anegre veneer tabletop by furniture artist Jack Larimore demonstrates one of the many impressive effects that can be generated with this technique.

Burl growths can occur at different places on trees, but typically they occur on the main trunk. Some species of trees also develop burls on the roots.

Due to their unusual growth pattern, burls present a wide variety of grain configurations. This group shows some of the available burl veneers.

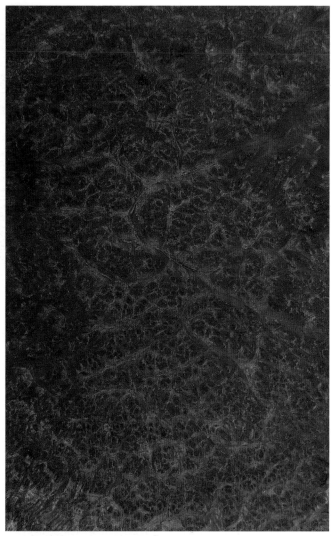

Amboyna burl is made up almost entirely of small buds or clusters.

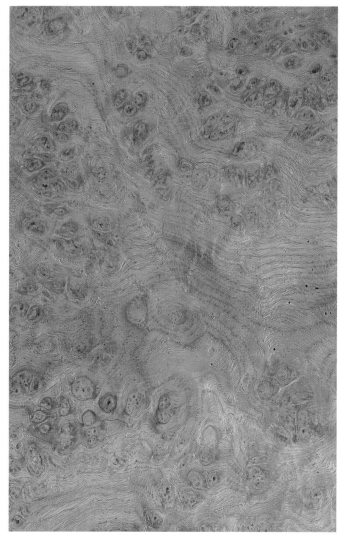

Olive ash burl demonstrates a more typical twisted and knotty burl pattern.

DEPICTION OF WOODEN SURFACES

When you depict the woodgrain of a particular species, there are certain elements you will have to consider and accurately represent if the deception is to be successful.

First, think about the color. While you have some latitude due to the conditions discussed previously, there are ranges you must stay within if you want the wood to be convincing. Strive for the correct tonal relationship between the light and dark growth rings and the appropriate overall color effect. Observe as many examples of the wood as you can to gain a feel for the structure and color.

Second, consider the nature of the grain pattern itself. The grain of some woods has a very prominent or jagged appearance while others have a more rounded or subtle form. And, of course, the way in which the lumber is cut from the log also affects the grain pattern.

Third, take note that the pore structure of certain woods is very prominent, while in others it is nonexistent.

Fourth, the structure of the wood can create moiré effects that appear as light and dark variations at cross angles to the grain. They are very distinctive in certain woods. If you represent these moirés effectively, you will greatly enhance your grain painting.

Finally, keep in mind that the sides and ends of boards also have grain patterns, and these surfaces will need to be represented correctly if exposed.

Some woods, such as oak and the ash shown here, will darken dramatically when exposed to water over a prolonged period.

Moirés are clearly visible at nearly right angles to the straight grain in this piece of anegre veneer.

The annual rings are clearly visible in the end grain of this flat-sawn board. If you were to paint the exposed end of such a board, you could reproduce a similar pattern. Straight-grain lumber, however, would not show the annual rings on the end but rather a light and dark series of straight lines at right angles to the board's surface.

The large pores of oak are easily observable in this multiboard panel. Notice that the combination of boards exhibits both heart- and straight-grain patterns.

materials *and tools*

In this chapter we'll discuss the materials and tools you'll need to achieve successful results in woodgraining. You'll learn the importance of priming and base painting, and I'll show you my best formulas for successful glazing recipes. I'll then walk you through the basics of tool selection and show you the varied results that each tool produces. Follow along with the information here and, when you get to the next chapter, you'll be set to tackle the actual graining process with unqualified success!

PAINTS AND GLAZES

Since grain painting generally consists of building up layers of paint, it is important that you know about the makeup of this layering technique. Different types of paint not only have distinct handling and drying characteristics but also may be affected by what is under or over them. Here is a list and brief description of the basic types of paint you need a thorough understanding of to be a successful grain painter. Keep in mind that paints give off fumes as they dry and cure. Read the product label for health and safety information, and always work in a well-ventilated area (preferably with forced air movement).

Primers

While you may be tempted to dismiss priming as an unnecessary chore, it's the first key to building a smooth, strong paint surface, without which you will not get good graining results. Priming seals back sap and stains in wood and provide a strong bond between the paint and raw material you are painting. By tinting your primer in the direction of the base coat, or using colored primer, you can build a richer base color more quickly. You may tint the primer yourself with universal tinting colors or have it done at the paint store.

There are three basic types of primers that you may find useful. Oil primers offer outstanding performance and relatively quick drying time. They flow out to a smooth finish and sand readily to remove excess brush marks. However, they require that you use paint thinner to clean your tools, and dry more slowly than some other primers.

Water-based primers have improved greatly over the last few years. They offer safety, convenience and quick drying time. Two major drawbacks come with the quick drying time. These primers retain more brush marks than oil primers, and they are somewhat difficult to sand. However, I have found that the William Zinsser & Co., Inc. brand Bulls Eye 1•2•3 primer does sand rather well. Also, 3M corporation makes a special sandpaper just for sanding latex paints and primers. If you want to lessen your exposure to the

Each of these three types of primer has its own advantages and performance characteristics. The Zinsser company makes all these, but your paint store may carry other acceptable brands.

fumes of paint thinner, water-based primer is worth investigating.

Shellac primers are alcohol based and offer sealing properties for difficult situations. They seal back sap and stains such as ink more effectively than the other primers. This may be especially helpful if you are working on used furniture that has ink or oily stains, or on very sappy wood such as knotty pine.

Base Paint

The paint that will form the first visible layer for your graining is base paint. As such, it will establish the underlying color for the final effect and must have the correct physical characteristics so you can achieve the desired results with the glazes you apply over it.

The standard choice for base coating is oil, or "alkyd" (the more accurate term), interior enamel. This type of paint, manufactured for the housepainting trade, is thinned with turpentine or paint thinner. It is relatively slow drying, but when dry is rather permanent and forms a nonporous film. It is available in a variety of sheens from flat to high gloss. Low gloss, eggshell and satin sheens usually are the best choices for grain painting.

Glazing Paints

Glazing paints are the paints you will use to create the color and figure of the wood-

Universal tinting colors may be added to primers to tint them closer to your base color. Your paint store can add them when you buy the primer, or you can purchase the colors and add them yourself.

grain. Depending on the circumstance, they can be either oil or water based. Each has its own advantages and applications.

Artists' Oil Paints

Artists' oil paints are high-quality, slow-drying paints that have a thick pastelike quality and are sold in tubes. You must thin them to a brushing consistency by adding turpentine, paint thinner or a painting medium that lends transparency and also makes them dry more quickly.

Many companies manufacture high-quality oil (alkyd) paints. Depending on their gloss and other characteristics, they will have different trade names. Many of the base colors listed as samples here are Benjamin Moore colors, designated by the letters B.M.

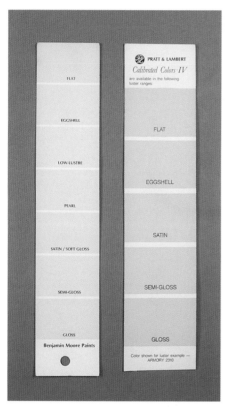

Manufacturers may have different names for degree of gloss. Here, two gloss charts show the range and steps used by Benjamin Moore, on the left, and Pratt & Lambert, on the right.

Like most artists' paints, these are sold by color names determined by specific pigment content. While the names are standard from brand to brand, higher quality paints will have more tinting strength and intense color. Buy artists' quality paints such as Grumbacher, Winsor & Newton, Utrecht or other nationally recognized brands.

why oil and not latex for base coating?

Latex house paint has received much attention in recent years as a safer, healthier and more convenient alternative to oil paint due to its lower emission of solvents, nonflammability and water cleanup. Manufacturers have worked very hard to improve its workability, and while they have been partially successful in their endeavors, it is important to understand that by its very nature, latex paint dries to a porous film. While this porosity is a good quality in certain applications, it is generally a detriment to the woodgrainer because the porous surface of the paint absorbs thinner from the glaze, thus causing the glaze to dry prematurely. The porous paint also may capture and hold pigment from the colored glaze you brush over it, causing undesirable streaking or staining. Due to this quality and its tendency to be difficult to sand, latex paint is generally a bad choice for base painting. However, If you are starting your work with a water glaze that will be sealed with either varnish or shellac before applying an oil overglaze, you may be able to get satisfactory results. If you wish to try this, I recommend an acrylic as opposed to latex house paint. One good choice would be the Muralo brand Ultra line of 100 percent acrylic house paint, which when fully cured has film characteristics similar to alkyd paint.

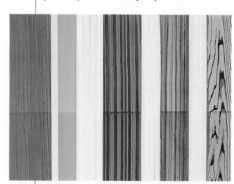

This chart shows the way glazes react when manipulated on the same color oil and latex paints. The top half of this board is coated with B.M. 194 Satin Impervo alkyd. The bottom half is coated with the same color, but it is latex enamel. The paint on the bottom panel has captured the pigment, thus giving a generally darker and less distinct result. The stripe second from left is the result of brushing on then wiping off the Burnt Sienna glaze. The staining of the latex enamel is very evident here.

Muralo Ultra brand house paint is a water-based acrylic emulsion paint that, when cured, behaves more like the oil paint on the top of the chart. If you have health or safety issues that prevent you from using oil paint, I recommend this as a viable alternative.

Artists' oil paints come in a variety of grades. Avoid student-grade paints as they aren't as permanent or stable as better grades. Purchase small tubes as they will go a long way when thinned with glaze medium.

This chart shows the colors you will need for the exercises in this book. While some grain painters prefer to nuance their work with a wider range of color, this palette will provide excellent results. From left to right the colors are: Raw Sienna, Burnt Umber, Cassel Brown (Cassel Earth), Mars Black, Prussian Blue, Alizarin Crimson, Burnt Sienna. While you should be able to find all these colors in artists' oil paints, you may have difficulty finding Cassel Brown, also referred to as Cassel Earth, in gouache. I purchase the dry pigment from the Kremer Pigments Company in New York City (see list of suppliers at the back of the book). An acceptable substitute for Cassel Brown can be made by mixing one part Burnt Umber and one part Mars Black, but the result will be less transparent than the genuine pigment. Not included in this chart, but useful in certain recipes, is Kramer Translucent Red #52400.

Water-Based Glazing Paint

Water-based paints can be either permanent or reversible. Both types dry quickly and are usually stable enough that you can apply oil glazes directly over them. This means that you can quickly create a two-layer finish by applying an oil glaze over a water-based one. The thin viscosity of water glazes allows you a wide range of manipulative technique.

Gouache is commercially prepared opaque artists' water-based paint sold in tubes. Do not confuse it with transparent artists' watercolor, which is a more expensive product. Thinning gouache with water creates a glaze that can be reworked or removed after it has dried. If you use gouache for graining, check the tubes to see if they are labeled as "permanent colors." Gouaches labeled as "designers colors" are not permanent, and such colors may fade rather quickly.

Vinegar paint is water-soluble paint you can make in the studio by mixing dry pigment with water, vinegar and a little soap. It is very economical and lasts indefinitely, and you can use any color pigment available. This is an advantage because some pigments are readily available in powder form that may be difficult if not impossible to find as ready-made paints.

Artists' acrylic paints are permanent water-based paints that may be used instead of gouache or vinegar paint for underglazing. However, once dry, acrylics cannot be removed or altered. I don't recommend them to beginners, but if you are

Gouache paints are generally sold in tubes like artists' oil colors. Since they are liable to dry out, be sure to close the tubes tightly.

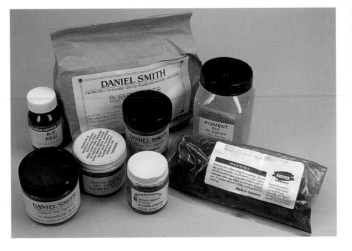

Dry pigments are sold by many art materials supply houses and are packaged differently by each. A small amount goes a long way.

This chart shows how the base color is revealed as the glaze becomes more transparent. As more medium is added, and as the glaze is brushed out, it becomes more transparent. From top to bottom, the colors are: Burnt Umber, Raw Sienna and Burnt Sienna.

sure of creating your desired effect, you may wish to try them. Since they are permanent, you do not need to seal them before going ahead with another glaze.

Glazes

A glaze is a thin transparent layer of paint. It may be created with either water-based or oil-based paint. A glaze may consist simply of pigment and a liquid, or it may have other ingredients added to enhance its handling characteristics. Oil glazes can be made using a variety of ingredients to thin the paint and make it transparent. Three types of oil glaze mediums are studio-made glaze mediums, premixed

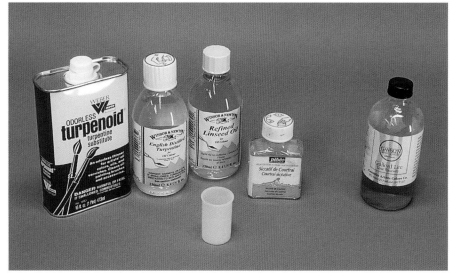

Here, on the left, are the ingredients needed to make an oil-paint glaze medium and, on the right, a ready-made alkyd medium. In front is a plastic 35mm film canister, a convenient measuring tool. The odorless turpentine substitute on the extreme left makes for a more pleasant work environment if you are sensitive to the odor of turpentine.

artists' alkyd glazing mediums and commercial housepainters' glazing liquid.

Studio-Made Glazes
Studio-made glaze medium recipes are plentiful and sometimes have exotic or unusual ingredients. But a good performing recipe can be made from a combination of artists' linseed oil, turpentine (or paint thinner) and a dryer to speed the setting of the paint film. The basic recipe is:
- one part artists' linseed oil
- three parts paint thinner or turpentine (add more paint thinner to make the glaze thinner, but it will also dry faster)
- no more than 10 percent dryer, also sold as siccative

The linseed oil will dry very slowly and bind the pigment particles together. The solvent (paint thinner or turpentine) will thin the medium to make it easier to brush and speed the drying. The dryer will further speed the final curing of the glaze so you can work over it without disturbing your already completed work. Glaze recipes suggesting other drying oils and solvents may be fine, but you will not find them necessary to accomplish the effects described in this book.

Studio-made mediums are the most traditional, and while they require you to mix the ingredients in the correct proportions,

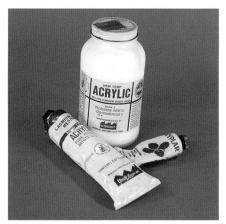

Artists' acrylic paints come in tubes and jars. The thinner paint sold in jars is easier to break down for glazes.

sealing water glazes

As mentioned before, you can work directly over dried water glaze with an oil glaze. But if you use strong rubbing or brushing action, you may disturb the dried water glaze and ruin your grain pattern. Prevent this from happening by sealing the water glaze with a coat of varnish or shellac before proceeding. Some of the techniques shown in this book suggest sealing the water glaze and some don't. As you gain experience, you will develop your own preference as to when you want to seal a water glaze and when you don't.

the dangers of linseed oil

Linseed oil generates heat as it dries. On the surface of a painting, this is not a problem; the heat easily dissipates. However, if you use a cloth or paper towel to wipe up linseed oil (or a glaze made from it) and throw it in a trash can where the heat becomes trapped, you will have created a potential fire hazard, as the cloth can spontaneously erupt in flames. Therefore, if you work with linseed oil glazes, use a fire-proof trash can, remove trash from your studio each night and spread out all affected cloths or paper towels so they can dry individually and freely.

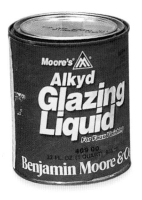

These housepainters' glaze mediums may be useful in certain situations but tend to dry rather quickly. On the left is an alkyd medium for oil paints and on the right are two latex glaze mediums.

you can tailor the mixture to your preferences by adjusting the recipe. For instance, you can extend or speed up drying times. One warning: You may be tempted to add more dryer to speed the process but doing so can result in the paint film eventually cracking. If you need to work very quickly, I suggest you consider one of the alkyd mediums described below.

Premixed Artists' Alkyd Glazes

The premixed artists' alkyd glazing mediums are higher quality than the housepainters' medium described below. They dry with a sheen and are transparent when wet, allowing you to see the true color of the glaze. Depending on their consistency, they can be thinned with mineral spirits or turpentine. These mediums set more quickly than the linseed-oil medium. As long as you have enough time to manipulate the glaze, a quicker drying time can be an advantage when working with furniture since you will have to handle the piece several different times. You can slow the drying time of some artists' alkyd mediums by adding a small amount (up to 10 percent) of linseed oil. Check the label.

Housepainters' Glaze

Commercial housepainters' glazing liquid is sold in paint stores to be mixed with oil or alkyd paints and paint thinner to create glazes for walls and woodwork. Because it

is made for walls, it dries flat. The flatting agent gives it a milky appearance while wet. As it is fairly inexpensive, this type of glaze can be useful if you need a large amount of a single color, but because it subtly changes the color of the paint while wet, you may find it difficult to adjust or judge colors accurately. You will also find that glaze made from this medium sets up very quickly, which can be a hindrance when you are trying to do multiple manipulations of the glaze over a large surface.

CLEAR COATINGS

Clear coatings such as shellac and varnish serve a variety of purposes. They seal, protect and enrich the color of your work.

Shellac

Shellac is a clear coating for which alcohol is the solvent. It dries quickly to a hard

nonporous finish, but unlike varnish it can be redissolved with solvent after it has set up. You can use it to seal a layer of paint or glaze so it will be unaffected by the next layer as you build up your grain painting. You can brush it on, but it's more convenient and less likely to disturb the underlying glaze if it is sprayed. Since it's widely available in spray cans, you can readily accomplish this, if you have good ventilation. Do not apply polyurethane directly over shellac; the two are incompatible.

Varnish

Varnish is a clear hard finish you will apply to complete the graining process. While it dries much more slowly than shellac, you can also use it to seal water glazes. Modern varnishes are either oil or water based. Water-based varnishes don't adhere very well to oil glazes and are gen-

working with water glazes

Water glazes for traditional grain painting require no additional ingredients other than the paint or pigment and water or vinegar to extend it. However, if you make your own water paint, you can add a small amount of glycerin or soap to improve adhesion and to slow the drying time. If you find that some pigments don't readily combine with water, you can add oxgall (a wetting agent) or a small amount of alcohol to aid in the initial mixing.

Keep in mind that water glazes made from gouache and studio-made paints are reversible and can be changed or cleaned off and redone even after they dry, while

glazes made from acrylic or latex paints are difficult, if not impossible, to remove once they have set up. If you must remove a dried acrylic glaze, alcohol will eventually dissolve the paint but an irreversible stain may be left behind.

While water-based glazes can be made from latex house paint and housepainters' water-based glazing liquid, these are generally not employed in traditional grain painting due to their very fast drying times and their propensity to hold brush marks. However, if you are willing to experiment, you might find them useful in some instances.

varnish: glossy or not?

Varnishes, like paints, can be purchased in a variety of sheens. To make varnish less shiny manufacturers add silica. This very fine granulated material causes the light to reflect at all different angles from the varnish, thus dulling it. The more silica added, the less shiny the varnish. I use gloss varnish for all my sealing and building coats, but since the graining process creates a textural surface as you work, a high-gloss finish may cause these textural qualities to be more noticeable. Therefore, I recommend that you either rub out the final finish to produce a softer sheen or you complete your finish with a final coat of semigloss varnish.

Polyurethane varnish, on the left, is my choice for finishing, but you may wish to use the more traditional alkyd varnish on the right. Each can be purchased with a range of surface gloss.

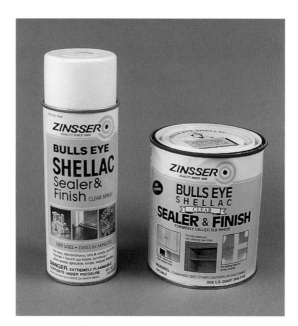

Shellac can be purchased in spray cans or as a brushable liquid. To seal graining surfaces, get clear, also referred to as white, shellac, not orange, which is much darker.

erally not employed in grain painting of furniture. While there are many types of oil-based varnish used in the fine arts field, you will want to choose between alkyd and polyurethane varnishes.

Alkyd varnish is chemically formulated in much the same way as alkyd paint, but it contains no pigment. It forms a durable protective film when dry, although it takes a relatively long time to do so. Generally 24 hours are required before you can recoat an alkyd varnish. Avoid varnishes sold as "quick drying," as they contain strong solvents that can dissolve thin glazes and the adhesive on tape.

Polyurethane varnish is thinned with mineral spirits like the alkyd varnish mentioned above but is chemically distinct and has different performance characteristics. Generally, it dries more quickly and has a tougher film than alkyd varnish, but it should not be applied directly over shellac. Therefore, if you use polyurethane to finish your graining, you should always make sure there is a barrier coat of some other oil-based glaze or varnish between it and any shellac you have applied. I generally prefer polyurethane to alkyd varnish and find that when applied according to manufacturer's directions, it gives the same visual results.

more about water-based varnishes

Water-based varnishes have the same basic physical attributes as water-based house paints with the same pros and cons. From a color standpoint though, they have one advantage over oil-based varnishes in that they dry without yellowing. All oil-based paints and varnishes will eventually yellow somewhat, but water-based products do not. Therefore, water-based varnishes are often recommended over very light finishes. Since most woods are not extremely light in color, and even those that are tend to be yellowish anyway, this nonyellowing quality is of limited advantage in graining. If you choose to use water-based varnish, keep in mind that in addition to limited bonding to oil glaze, it will dry very quickly and may leave more brush marks than oil-based varnish.

TOOLS

Throughout history, artists and craftsmen have created tools to help them depict the visual qualities of wood. Some of these tools are manufactured and somewhat expensive while others are homemade and inexpensive. In some cases you can improvise and achieve acceptable results by replacing the expensive tool with an adaptation of a cheaper one. However, if you do this, your results may be more time-consuming and difficult to achieve.

General Use Brushes

For most people, brushes are simply a means to apply a smooth coat of paint. But for the woodworker, restorer or decorative artist, they have a variety of other functions. Their size, form and bristle material are directly tied to their function. For example, flat brushes are good for use on both smooth and complex surfaces. They come in a variety of sizes, but for applying paint or varnish on furniture, I rarely use anything larger than 2".

Round brushes are handy when dealing with uneven or curving surfaces and are good for applying glazes. Angled brushes allow you to work with your hand at a more relaxed angle and are good for reaching into corners.

Lastly, foam brushes work great on flat surfaces and eliminate conventional brush marks, and special varnish brushes, made with fine bristles, allow you to apply a smoother coat of varnish.

natural or synthetic?

When you are applying a coat of paint onto a surface, natural bristle brushes perform better for oil-based paint and nylon bristle brushes perform better with water-based paint, such as latex. There are some exceptions to this rule, but it is particularly true when you are priming or base coating.

Brushes for applying paint take various shapes and are made from both natural and man-made materials. Pictured from left to right: 2" foam, 2" nylon bristle flat, $7/8$" natural bristle round, No. 2 natural bristle oval sash, 1" slanted natural bristle flat and a badger-hair varnish brush.

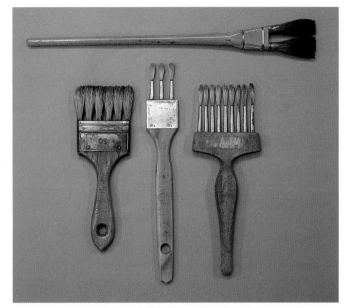

These special brushes have split bristles to create a striped application. From left to right: toothed spalter, small pencil over-grainer, and larger pencil over-grainer, all with hog bristles. Above them is a squirrel-hair double header.

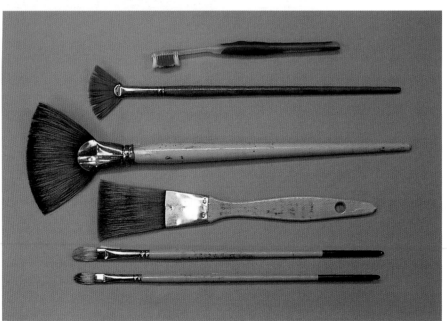

Shown here are special application brushes. From top to bottom: toothbrush for speckling, small and large fan brushes for blending or softening, veinette for creating fine straight grain and artists' oil filberts for drawing heart grain.

Specialty Brushes and Functions

Certain brushes allow you to put on paint in specific ways or create other effects after the paint has been applied. For example, once you have applied paint, you may use a particular brush to spread out an even layer, to create a texture or pattern or to move paint around to construct moiré effects. You never apply paint with these brushes. And though you need to keep all your brushes clean, these brushes must be maintained immaculately.

Natural Bristle Spalters

These short-bristle brushes are ideal for evening out glaze after you have applied it to the surface. You will also use them to draw heart grain and create moirés. Although they are natural bristle brushes, you will use them for both oil- and water-based techniques. Some grainers maintain separate sets for each medium.

Flogger and Mottler

The flogger brush makes a series of marks resembling the pores of wood when you pat it on the surface of wet paint. You can also drag it through a thin glaze to create linear effects. The mottler, on the other hand, is used to create moiré patterns, such as those found in bird's-eye maple. By gripping a spalter's bristles to curve them, you can achieve similar effects.

Blenders, Badgers and Cod Tails

These brushes with odd-sounding names are essential to creating the blended effects you'll so often see in woodgraining. Blending brushes are used to pull colors together or to soften an edge or pattern. Only specially constructed brushes will do the job, and while they are expensive, there really is no other way to achieve the effect. Badgers allow you to soften wet edges and pull colors together, and the cod-tail brush is used to blend heavier oil-based glazes.

Brushes used to manipulate paint that is already on the surface come in many forms. These short-bristle brushes are called spalters or mottlers. The small one is 1½", medium is 3" and the large is 4" wide.

Pictured here on the left is a flogger, and on the right is a wavy mottler. Keep in mind that these special brushes are never dipped into paint but are only used to move the paint around on the surface.

The bristle blender on the left is used with oil glazes while the badger-hair blender on the right is primarily for water media.

Graining Tools

Besides brushes, a variety of other tools will help you create paint effects that will simulate the pattern of the grain lines, pore structure and moirés. Most are used to remove paint that is already on the surface. Here is a list of some things you can use, though you may discover others that you can make or buy.

Graining Combs

These versatile tools give you the power to duplicate grain. Each type has a specific function: Steel combs are dragged through oil glazes to create finely spaced grain lines. Rubber and cardboard combs allow you to create straight-grain lines in either water or oil glazes.

Rubber Grain Rockers

Mounted and molded rockers are used to create a pattern for repetitive heart grain. Sheet rockers are wrapped around a can or cylinder to take advantage of the irregularities in their patterning.

Additional Texturing Tools

The kinds of tools you can come up with for graining are almost endless, as so many items can be used effectively. Some of the items I keep handy are:

- sea sponges
- cellulose sponges
- pleated plastic
- steel wool and scrubbing pads
- burlap and other textiles
- cotton swabs

Graining combs come in a variety of incarnations. On the left are two cardboard combs. Next is a graduated rubber comb, a triangular rubber comb, and several metal combs that are sold as a set.

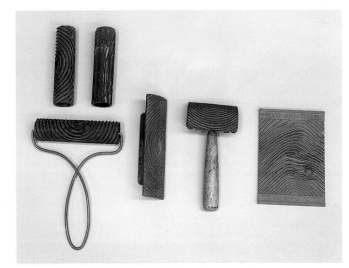

Rubber graining rockers allow you to create heart-grain patterns. The three on the left are a cylindrical set that attach to the wire handle, the next two are curved rockers and the last is a molded flat sheet that you wrap around a can.

Miscellaneous painting tools include burlap, plastic wrap, cotton swabs, sea sponge, cellulose sponge, steel wool and a scrubbing pad.

A check roller is used to add large pores for oak.

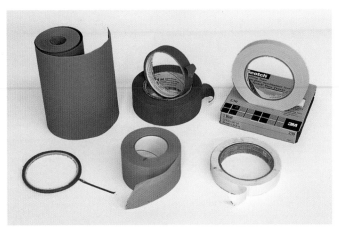

Taping materials include: masking paper, painters' tape, drafting tape for more sensitive areas or where you need to leave the tape on for an extended period, low-tack tape for really delicate work, wider painters' tape and 1/8" automotive tape.

Tapes

You will use a variety of tapes to help create convincing joints, edges and other details. Drafting tape is my favorite. It looks like masking tape but performs much better. It has a heavier body so it resists tearing and is less sticky. It also tends to be less reactive to paint and glaze film than any other tape I have used. It also breaks down much more slowly, which means you can leave it on the surface longer. It is more expensive than painters' tape but performs better. Do not attempt to use standard masking tape as it will destroy your work by pulling up paint and leaving a sticky residue behind.

Painters' tape comes in a variety of colors and widths. For delicate work, for instance, when you have built up layers of glaze and there is a risk of pulling it up when you remove the tape, use the least sticky tape available. When you need wider protection, there are wider tapes. Even these special tapes can react with varnishes or glaze and pull up your surface, so never apply them to an uncured surface and always remove them slowly and carefully.

Automotive masking tape is specially made for auto body shops and is not destructive like standard masking tape. It comes in a variety of widths. I find the ⅛" wide to be the most versatile. This tape will allow you to create inlaid lines.

creating sharp corners with tape

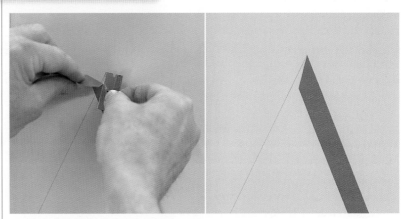

1 Draw the shape you wish to tape, then lay the tape next to it and press it down. At the end of the shape, position a razor blade against the tape and tear the tape up against the blade leaving a crisp edge.

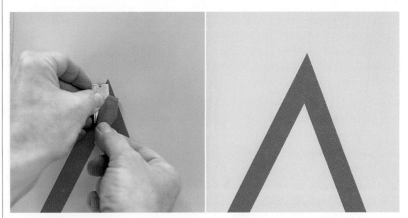

2 Repeat the process on the other side of the shape, making sure to overlap the ends. This will leave a perfectly formed corner with no damage to the surface and a minimum of wasted tape.

3 When adding a new section beside a finished area, make sure that the tape is set back from the edge so there is a slight overlap of the painted surfaces. A darker line between boards or pieces of veneer is always more aesthetic than a line of the base color.

Miscellaneous Tools and Materials

There are other tools and materials you will need from time to time:

- Tack cloths clean dust from surfaces to be painted.
- Cans and bottles are for mixing paints and other mediums.
- Cheesecloth and cotton rags aid in touch-ups and cleanup.
- A drafting compass will help draw borders and determine equal spacing without measuring.
- A palette can be purchased or home-made. It should be smooth, non-porous, light in color and big enough to mix a few colors at once, at least a foot square. Glass, plastic, varnished wood or coated paper may be used.
- A palette knife helps begin the mixing process of thick artists' paints.
- A lining tool allows you to create lines of various widths, in particular, those that mimic inlay around the edges of doors, drawers and tabletops.
- Sandpaper comes in various grades of extrafine, fine, medium and coarse. Use coarse papers of 100 and 125 grit to remove rough spots from raw wood or already painted surfaces. Use medium grades of 150 to 220 grit to finish sanding raw wood and to sand primers and base coats. Fine grades of 240 to 350 grit may be used to smooth a final coat of base paint. Very fine grades of 400 to 1,200 grit are used with water lubrication to sand varnish between coats and remove any imperfections from the final varnish.
- Lightweight paperboard is needed for painting samples. Called railroad board, it's coated with clay on one side and often available at art supply stores that cater to the sign painting trade.
- Whiting is used like cleanser to make oil-painted surfaces ready to receive water glazes and to reduce the tendency of tape to permanently bond to freshly painted surfaces.
- Rubbing compounds aid in the final finishing to create a smooth blemish-free surface.
- Paste wax adds a final layer of protection to finished surfaces. It helps make drawers and doors open smoothly.

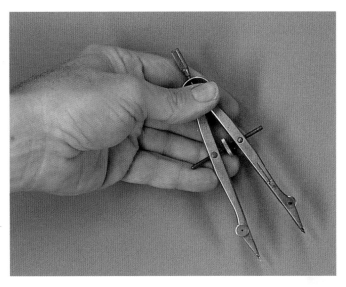

A drafting compass allows you to draw consistent borders by hooking one side over the edge of a piece of furniture and pulling it along the length. It is also handy for comparing sizes or marking intervals without measuring.

A paper palette tablet is handy because it enables you to easily and quickly attain a clean surface to mix your paints and glazes. Pictured to the left of the paper palette tablet is a glass palette made by taping white paper to the back of a piece of plate glass.

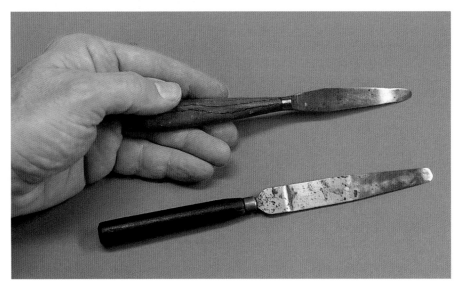

Use a palette knife to break down and blend the stiff oil paint with other colors or mediums.

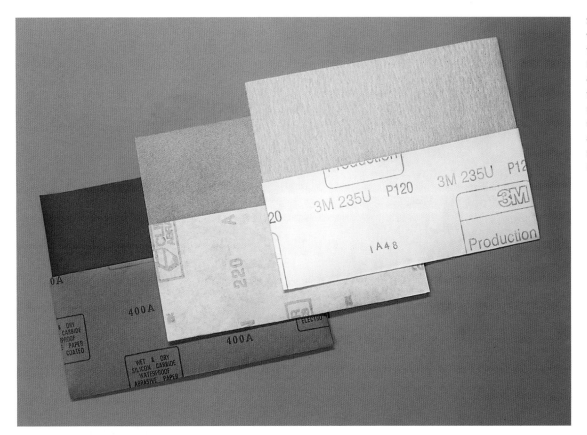

Sandpaper comes in a wide range of materials for special uses. On the left is fine paper that can be used with water, the center piece is a medium-grade paper for sanding wood or paint and on the right is a special paper for sanding latex paint.

A lining tool allows you to add inlay lines for emphasis and color variation.

Use a tack cloth after you have sanded or to clean any dust from the surface prior to painting or varnishing.

woodgraining *techniques*

Grain painting, while beautiful, can be labor intensive. The results you achieve are directly proportional to your understanding of the visual effect you're attempting to duplicate. Go out and find examples of specific woods you can use as models, and then practice until you have the effect committed to memory. Just as important as having those models is understanding the techniques involved in duplicating the look you want to achieve. In this chapter, I'll show you the general techniques used in woodgraining. Don't get impatient and jump ahead to see how specific species are done. Practice these general techniques, and you'll be well prepared for what comes next — the duplication of specific species.

PREPARING THE SURFACE

Every successful grain-painting project starts with careful surface preparation. You need a very smooth surface with a consistent, appropriate coloration. It must also be nonporous and have a low gloss. Assuming you are starting with raw wood, the steps for proper surface prep are:

- Check the surface for gouges, chips or holes that you must fill with spackling paste or other repair material.
- After the filler has hardened, sand with coarse sandpaper (100 to 125 grit) to remove milling marks, excess filler or other minor surface defects. Always sand in the direction of the grain of the wood — sanding across the grain will impart scratches.
- Sand with medium sandpaper (150 to 175 grit) to remove the marks left by the first sanding.
- Prime the surface with either an oil- or water-based primer. Water-based primers are more convenient. Oil-based primers, however, will flow out better and require less sanding. While primers are usually sold in white, you can have your primer tinted closer to the color of your base coat at the paint store.
- When the primer is dry, examine the surface carefully for defects. Fill any blemishes that are still visible, then sand with medium sandpaper again to smooth the filler.
- Base coat with the appropriate oil-based paint. Flatter paints sand more easily and will take a water glaze more readily. If you are working directly over the base coat with oil glaze, however, a satin finish oil paint is fine.
- When the base coat dries, which may take 24 hours or so, sand with fine sandpaper (200 to 220 grit). If you see runs or curtains, allow them to dry more thoroughly before sanding them out completely. Drips or sags left on the surface will prevent you from achieving the desired effect.
- Base coat again. When this coat dries, you should have a smooth, uniform surface on which to proceed.

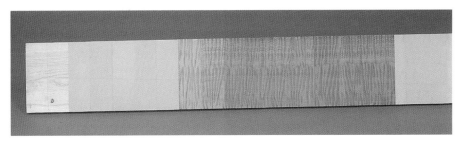

ALL PROCESS SAMPLE BOARD

This pine board shows the steps necessary to go from raw wood to a grained and finely finished varnish surface. Keep in mind that each section is representative of a procedure that has been applied not only to the exposed section but to the entire grained area to its right. The sections from left to right show: raw wood, sanded wood, primed surface, sanded primer, first base coat, sanded base coat, second base coat, first water glaze grain layer, second water glaze grain layer, oil glaze toning layer, subsequent varnish coats alternated with the sanded varnish surface, culminating in a very uniform, smooth satin finish.

proper degreasing

Deglossing or degreasing is a necessary process when you apply a water glaze over any nonporous surface. Water-based paint tends to bead up, or ciss, on oil paint, varnish or shellac. Deglossing is accomplished by rubbing the surface with a damp sponge and a little whiting. This removes any oil residue from the surface and creates a minute scratch pattern that eliminates the beading and allows you to manipulate the water glaze on the surface. If the surface is "tender," say only a coat of shellac, then dusting on a coating of whiting will suffice.

When water or vinegar glaze is brushed over a newly dried oil-base coat, the oil resists the water and results in beading or cissing.

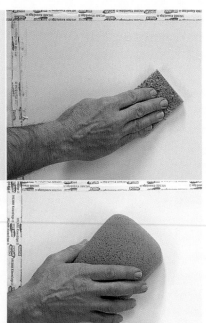

Degreasing the surface of an oil-base coat is accomplished with whiting and a damp sponge. Sprinkle the whiting on the sponge and thoroughly scrub the surface. After scrubbing, use a clean sponge and remove the whiting paste from the surface. Water glaze will now lay smoothly on the surface and can be manipulated and textured as you wish.

GLAZE RECIPES

Before you attempt to produce woodgrain effects on a finished piece, you should practice on sample boards with the individual tools and brushes to get a feel for how they work. Try all of your procedures with both oil and water glazes to see how each responds.

Oil Glaze Recipes

You can prepare an oil glaze medium in any of the following ways, using either artists' oil paint or alkyd house paint.

Recipe One

Mix paint with ready-made artists' alkyd oil painting medium. Add mineral spirits to the glaze to thin the consistency and speed the drying time, or linseed oil to slow the drying. Consult the label on the glaze container for recommendations. The glaze color should be strong enough to impart its character without obscuring any underlying figure. When you brush out the glaze, it should spread to produce an even coat of color with few or no brush marks. Aim for the quality of a sheet of stained glass. Test your glaze for translucency by brushing it out on a sample board. Some colors have greater tinting strength and require more medium to create the desired effect.

Recipe Two

Mix paint with a medium of one part linseed oil to three to five parts turpentine or paint thinner, plus 5 to 10 percent dryer (siccative). Mix the medium ingredients together first, then add to the paint. Using artists' quality materials for this recipe may cost more but will give better and longer lasting results. Besides giving you more range in establishing the glaze consistency, this recipe has the added benefit of producing a slower drying medium, especially if you reduce the amount of dryer. A longer drying time can help you achieve more complex effects where you need to manipulate the glaze before it dries.

how to make a sample board

You will need to make several sample boards to practice on and to test colors. My preferred way to do this is to cut pieces of 1"-thick rigid foam insulation into drawing-board-size pieces and tape clay-coated railroad board to them. The coated railroad board, which becomes the actual sample, makes a great surface to paint on, and the lightweight foam insulation is a stiff, cheap and easy-to-handle support. After you have base painted the boards, they can be easily moved and stacked vertically to save space.

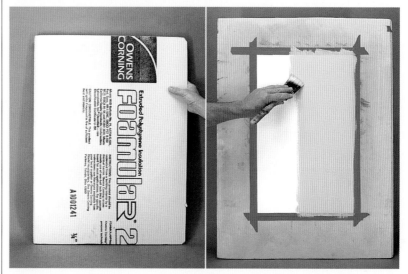

Foam insulation board makes a great support for sample boards. Tape the railroad board to the foam board, then apply your base coat. This allows you to work vertically and to stack the boards more conveniently.

Recipe Three

Mix the paint with housepainters' alkyd glaze medium and paint thinner. First, mix the medium and thinner together in a proportion of one part glaze medium to one part thinner, then add your paint. If you use house paint for your glaze, add about one part paint to make a glaze. If you are using artists' oil paints, you will need much less paint due to the strength of the colors. This glaze will dry rather quickly so it is not appropriate where you need time to manipulate the wet glaze.

Water Glaze Recipes

Water glazes are either removable or permanent. Permanent glazes won't be disturbed if you work over them with another glaze, whereas removable water glazes are susceptible to disruption if you work over them. But removable glazes give you greater flexibility since they can be altered even after they have dried. All of the water glazes I use are the impermanent type because I like their simplicity and flexibility, but you may want to try permanent water glazes in some recipes once you become familiar with the processes.

You can make impermanent water glazes from either of the two following recipes. Note that both these water glaze mixtures require constant stirring as the pigment readily sinks to the bottom of the container.

Recipe One

Purchase artists' gouache in tubes like artists' oil color, and mix it with water to create a liquid. It will not run if you lay it out with a spalter on a vertical surface. Because water glaze is a mixture, not a solution, you must constantly stir it to keep the pigment from settling on the bottom. For this reason, I make up only what I can use in a day's time. Stirring a big pail of glaze becomes tiring very quickly.

Recipe Two

Purchase powdered pigment and mix it with apple-cider vinegar and a dash of liquid dish detergent (⅛ tsp. detergent in 8 oz. of vinegar). Mix about two parts vinegar to one part dry pigment. Some pigments will require more or less liquid to form a glaze. This mixture will behave similarly to the gouache. However, I prefer it to gouache for its economy and versatility. I find that mixing color recipes with dry pigments is more exact and easier than messing with tubes of gouache. In addition, tubes tend to dry out before I use all the paint. Also there are some colors that I can buy as dry pigment that I cannot find as a gouache.

mixing oil paint and medium to create a glaze

1 On a palette or in a large, flat container, place the chosen color(s) of artists' oil paint.

2 Use a palette knife to begin the mixing.

3 Add a small amount of medium and mix it into the paint.

4 Continue to mix the medium and paint until you achieve the desired consistency. At this point, you could begin to manipulate the glaze with a brush and complete the mixing process by adding additional medium or solvent.

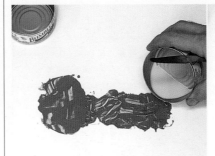

5 For comparison, mix some of the paint with the housepainters' glaze medium in a similar fashion. The results will be similar, but due to the flatting agent in the glaze medium, the glaze will be less transparent and slightly lighter than the other glaze.

MAKING A GLAZE FROM DRY PIGMENT

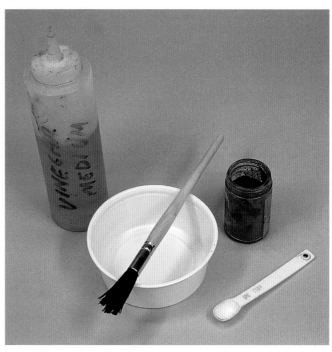

Mixing a water glaze from dry pigment requires only a few ingredients and simple tools. Apple-cider vinegar and some dish detergent (a half-pint of vinegar and ⅛ tsp. of detergent) are combined to create the medium. The dry pigment is the coloring agent. A little alcohol can be added if necessary to help dissolve the pigment.

I use a plastic deli container to mix vinegar glaze.

1 Measure the pigment with a measuring spoon or other measuring tool, depending on how much you need. Then add approximately twice as much medium as pigment.

2 Stir vigorously with the No. 2 oval sash brush.

APPLYING A GLAZE STEP-BY-STEP

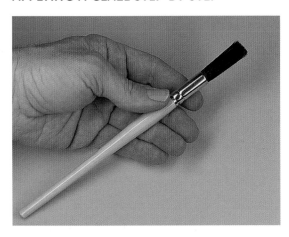

To begin the graining application, you first have to apply the glaze. I use relatively small (No. 2) natural bristle, oval sash brushes because the surface areas of furniture are usually not very large. After the glaze is on the surface, use a small spalter to redistribute it.

1 After you have thoroughly mixed your glaze, brush it onto the surface.

2 Take a spalter brush across the application to begin to even out the layer.

3 Brush in the direction of the application to finish off. This readies the glaze for texturing.

4 If you get too much oil glaze on the surface, you can remove some of it by dabbing with a wad of cheesecloth. Do this quickly. The glaze will begin to set up once you open up the surface with the cheesecloth.

Zebrawood is a good example of a straight-grain wood.

Macassar ebony is also straight grained.

CREATING STRAIGHT GRAIN

Many woods have some element of straight grain in them. The types of tools you can use to produce straight grain are almost endless. In most instances you'll produce the grain by pulling the tool through wet glaze to create a pattern of lines. Graining combs, sponges, steel wool and various textiles are some of the most common materials used to achieve straight grain. You can even make your own combs by tearing paperboard. When creating straight grain, observe the following guidelines:

- Maintain consistent pressure on the tool.
- Move the tool in a straight line by pulling it toward you.
- On larger surfaces, bend forward and reach out as far as possible to avoid running out of room as you pull the tool toward yourself. If you have to stop to take a step backward, a "hiccup" will form in the grain.
- When possible, start the movement of the tool in front of where you wish it to actually begin and finish by covering the area you want to grain without stopping.

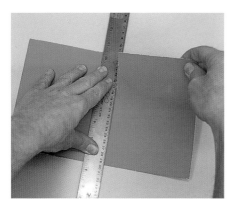

CREATING A STRAIGHT-GRAINING COMB
Make a graining comb for fine straight grain by simply tearing a piece of railroad board against a straightedge. This piece has been painted so you can see the resulting deckled edge that will produce comb lines. For a coarser grain, cut teeth into the comb.

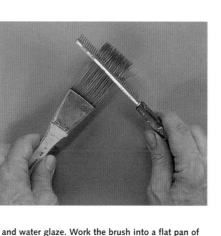

USING A VEINETTE BRUSH TO APPLY GLAZE
You can also brush on straight grain using a veinette brush and water glaze. Work the brush into a flat pan of glaze, as shown in the left photo. Then, as shown in the middle photo, comb through the wet brush with a fine comb such as a metal pet comb or brush-cleaning comb. This will separate the bristles and allow you to lay on a series of very fine lines, as shown in the right-hand photo.

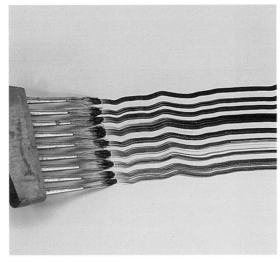

PENCIL OVER-GRAINER EFFECTS
Use a pencil over-grainer if you are working in oil glazes.

TORN CARDBOARD COMB EFFECTS
Here is an example of straight grain with a torn cardboard comb.

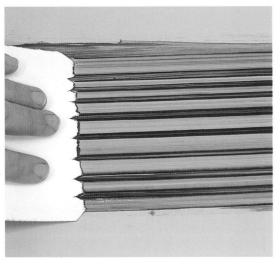

NOTCHED CARDBOARD COMB EFFECTS
Here is an example of straight grain with a notched cardboard comb.

STEEL WOOL EFFECTS
Here is an example of straight grain with steel wool.

RUBBER GRAINER EFFECTS
Here is an example of straight grain with a graduated rubber grainer.

CELLULOSE SPONGE EFFECTS
Here is an example of straight grain with a cellulose sponge.

CREATING HEART GRAIN

Heart grain, cut near the center of the tree, exhibits a series of V-shaped lines, a distortion of the annual rings. For smaller areas, an easy way to create regular heart grain is to use a graining rocker. More complex and irregular heart-grain patterns will have to be painted with brushes.

You can create heart-grain patterns with a rubber graining rocker by pulling it through the paint. Different rockers will give different grain patterns as will the speed with which you raise and lower the tool while moving it.

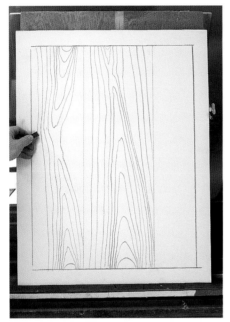

Practice drawing the different heart-grain patterns of specific woods on paper. This will prepare you for attacking them with paint.

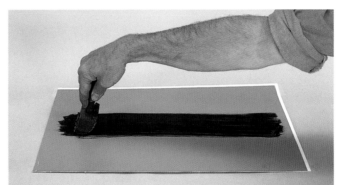

1 Begin with the grain rocker held far out in front of you with the handle in a near-vertical position.

2 Pull the rocker toward you slowly and smoothly, lowering the handle while keeping consistent pressure on the surface.

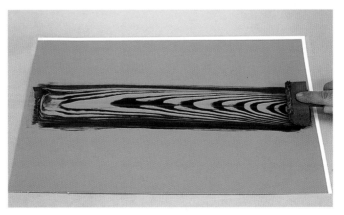

3 Finish with the rocker handle nearly horizontal to the surface. If the surface is very long, you can begin to lift the handle and continue to pull and the Vs will continue in the opposite direction.

CREATING PORES

There are a variety of ways to create the pore structure of wood, depending on the size, placement and prevalence of the pores. In woods in which the pores are large and widespread but not so prominent, you can create the pores as a first step, referred to as an underglaze. After brushing on a thin water glaze of the correct color, use the flogging brush to strike the entire surface. This creates an overall textural effect appropriate for woods such as walnut and mahogany.

For woods with small pores, you can add them later by spattering them on. Use a toothbrush or other stiff brush to create the specks, then elongate them with a blending brush or spalter.

For oak, in which the pores are very prominent and large, there is a special tool called a check roller that allows you to roll on the pores (see page 26 for photo). The trick with this tool is to get the correct amount of glaze onto the roller by tapping the wheels with a loaded brush as you roll it along.

The general goal when creating pores is to aim for overall consistency.

By striking the surface with a flogger after you have applied the glaze, you can create a general large-pore pattern. Start at the bottom of the panel and work up in single file, hitting the surface with the side of the brush.

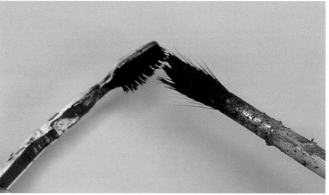

1 To create small pores, first apply glaze to a toothbrush.

2 Flick the toothbrush with a craft stick to distribute the glaze.

3 Brush the speckles into oblong spots with a blending brush.

CREATING MOIRÉS

Moirés are created due to the way the structure of the wood reflects light. They seem to appear and disappear at nearly right angles to the main direction of the grain. Though your painted moirés will not move or change color as the observer changes his position, you can achieve a high degree of realism by using a combination of the techniques demonstrated here.

method *one*

Make smaller moirés with torn cardboard. You can use this type for oak.

Press a torn piece of cardboard into a wet oil glaze to make smaller moirés. The moirés should be slightly oblique to the main direction of the grain.

method *two*

Use a wavy mottler or a spalter held in a curved grip to "walk" through a water glaze to make a wavy or curly moiré effect. This is the first step in achieving the "bird's-eye" grain.

A wavy mottler is a great tool for making the moirés underlying grains, such as bird's-eye maple.

If you don't have a wavy mottler, you can accomplish the same effect by holding a large spalter in the manner pictured to depress the center of the bristles.

Start at the top of a glazed panel and "walk" the wavy mottler down the board by moving one end and then the other like a drunken sailor wobbling down the pier. The same motion is used while holding the large spalter in the arced grip as pictured. The results are very similar.

method *three*

Use a softening brush held in a curved grip to sweep the wet glaze up and down, creating a double arc of glaze. This is generally combined with the sharp removal of two "eyes" on either side of the "butterfly." This type of moiré is created by nearby knots.

  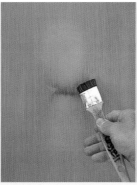 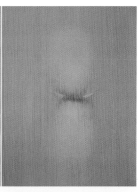

1 Another more individualistic type of moiré is often seen near knots. To make this type of effect, take a blending brush and sweep down the glaze.

2 Sweep back up in the same area to create an arc and an inverted arc close together.

3 Use a damp short-bristle flat brush to touch in two eyes on either side of the double arc.

4 When completed, your effect will look something like this.

method *four*

Press a piece of pleated plastic into the wet glaze to create a series of close lines at right angles to the main direction of the grain. This makes very tight moirés characteristic of fiddleback or tiger maple.

With a piece of pleated plastic wrap, you can make long moirés like those seen in fiddleback or tiger maple. While keeping the material stretched taut, press it into the wet glaze, overlapping each mark with the next.

method *five*

Use metal graining combs to make overlapping strokes, which help create the type of moirés often seen in oak.

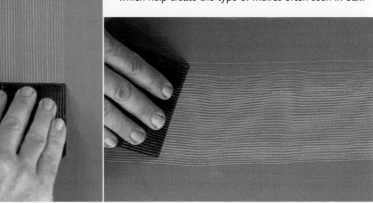

A very optical moiré, sometimes seen in oak, can be made using metal combs. Pull a fine metal comb through the wet glaze to create straight parallel lines. Keep the direction or the end of this comb perpendicular to the direction of the grain lines. Then choose a slightly wider comb and pull it over the same area, holding the comb at a slightly oblique angle to the direction of the grain. Viola! You will have a very complex-looking moiré.

VARNISHING

While not a graining technique per se, you will need to apply varnish either to seal layers of your graining or to protect your work when complete. By following some basic procedures, you can ensure the quality of your work.

- Purchase high-quality varnish from a reputable manufacturer such as Minwax, Waterlox, Pratt & Lambert, McCloskey or Benjamin Moore.
- Use a high-quality varnish brush that is absolutely clean.
- Apply varnish over thoroughly dried paint or varnish.
- Always clean the surface with a tack cloth immediately before varnishing.
- To ensure good coverage, initially brush the varnish across the direction of the grain. Always finish by brushing out in the direction of the grain.
- Sanding with fine sandpaper (400 to 600 grit) between coats will assure a smoother finish and better adhesion; however, do not sand the first coat of varnish applied over a grained surface. If you do so, you are very likely to sand through the varnish and remove some of your graining work.

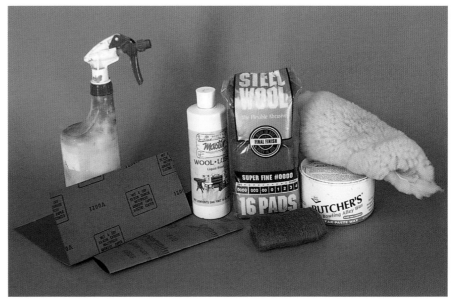

VARNISHING SUPPLIES

These are the supplies you will need to accomplish a smooth, blemish-free finish: a spray bottle filled with water and a little soap, fine and very fine wet/dry sandpaper, Behlen's Wool Lube, #0000 grade steel wool, paste wax and a lamb's wool buffing pad.

final varnishing step-by-step

If the final glaze was an oil glaze, then you should make sure the surface is clean by going over the surface lightly with a tack cloth to remove dust particles that may have settled on it while drying. If the final glaze was a water glaze, you can varnish as soon as it dries.

1. Before you varnish, be sure to clean the surface with a tack cloth. Even if you have not sanded, there will be dust on the surface, and it will mar your finish.
2. Lay a liberal coat of varnish across the grain.
3. Immediately brush out the varnish in the direction of the grain and let dry.
4. Repeat the first three steps for a second coat and let dry.
5. Sand lightly in the direction of the grain with 400-grit paper.
6. Repeat steps 1, 2 and 3 for a third coat.
7. Sand carefully with 400-grit paper lubricated with water, then wipe the area clean.
8. Apply fourth coat of varnish. If you wish to stop with this coat, applying satin varnish will help obscure minor imperfections and give a more subdued finish. If you wish to continue the process for a finer finish, you may continue to apply coats of gloss varnish, sanding with finer water lubricated papers, up to 1,200 grit, as you go.
9. Rub out the last coat of gloss varnish with #0000 grade steel wool and Behlen's Wool Lube to even out and subdue the gloss.
10. Finally, apply a coat of paste wax and buff it with a piece of lamb's wool, always working in the direction of the grain.

creating specific *species of woods*

This chapter shows you how to create several different woodgrains. Some depend primarily on tools to create the effects, and some require drawing skills to achieve the desired result. Depending on your experience and capabilities, you may want to begin with the tool-dependent techniques and work up to the techniques that require drawing-oriented skills.

CREATING LIGHT OAK

You can change the tone of this oak grain by adjusting the base color. A pale straw color is the most common base.

MATERIALS LIST

Sample board coated with low-luster, pale straw oil paint, B.M. (Benjamin Moore) 194 or similar

Palette and/or containers for glazes

Water glazes
- Glaze No. 1: four parts Raw Sienna to one part Burnt Umber
- Glaze No. 2: three parts Raw Sienna to one part Burnt Umber

Oil glaze: three parts Raw Sienna to one part Burnt Umber

Two No. 2 natural bristle oval sash brushes for glaze application

Small and medium spalters

Badger blender and cod-tail oil blender

Foam brush or other flat brush

Graining rocker

Check roller

Graduated rubber graining comb

Torn cardboard for moirés

Paint thinner for cleanup

1 | Orient the sample so that the brush strokes are going the direction in which you will paint the grain. Quickly brush on the water glaze No. 1 with a natural bristle No. 2 oval sash brush.

2 | Use a medium-size spalter to lay out the glaze. First, stroke across the grain direction and then finish off stroking with the grain direction. You may have to do this a couple times to get an even distribution. You should be able to see the color of the base paint through the glaze. If your glaze is too thick, or you put too much on, you will not get the transparent effect necessary.

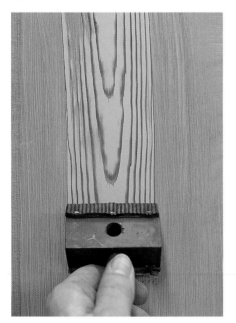

3 | Use the graining rocker to create a heart pattern near but not directly in the middle of the panel.

4 | With the badger blender, immediately whisk out the Vs only in the direction they point.

5 | Use the graduated rubber graining comb to add straight grain on one side of the heart grain. Hold the comb so that the lines get closer as they get farther from the heart grain.

6 | Soften the lines with the badger brush. Then repeat these steps on the other side of the heart grain to finish the board. If you have to make a second pass with the rubber graining comb to finish the area, be careful to not overlap, just go alongside. Do all this quickly as the water glaze will dry within a few minutes.

7 | As soon as the grain dries, use the check roller and the water glaze No. 2 to lay in the pores. A foam brush works well for applying the glaze to the check roller, but a bristle brush will also work. If you don't get enough pores in with one pass, make another try. If the pores look too harsh, they may also be softened in the same fashion as the grain.

8 | When the pores dry, brush on the oil glaze.

9 | Use a small spalter to lay out the glaze, as always finishing up in the direction of the grain.

10 | Press a piece of torn railroad board into the wet oil glaze on one side of the heart grain to create a series of moirés.

11 | Soften the moirés with a cod-tail oil blender to complete the sample.

CREATING MACASSAR EBONY

This wood is usually available as veneer. It was popular during the Art Deco period. Besides the black parts, it has a range of color from warm brown to a bright cinnamon. This sample falls into the bright end of the range.

MATERIALS LIST

Sample board coated with low-luster brown-orange oil paint, B.M. (Benjamin Moore) 028 or similar

Palette and/or containers for glazes

Water glaze: black

Oil glaze: Burnt Umber

Torn and cut cardboard combs

Badger blender

Toothbrush for spattering

Two No. 2 oval sash brushes for glaze application

Small and medium spalters

Paint thinner for cleanup

1 | Lay a black water glaze onto a medium brown-orange board.

2 | Lay out the glaze with a medium spalter. Go across first then in the direction of the grain.

3 | Pull a torn and cut cardboard comb through the glaze to create the strong parallel strokes of this wood.

4 | Use a badger brush to soften the grain, moving it at a very slight angle to the direction of the grain.

5 | Use a toothbrush to spatter the pore structure onto the surface. Do a small section at a time.

6 | After you spatter a section, use the badger brush to soften in the direction of the grain.

7 | Brush on the Burnt Umber glaze.

8 | Finish the sample by evening out the oil glaze with a small spalter.

CREATING BIRD'S-EYE MAPLE

While this is also a three-layer technique, the execution of each layer is a bit more complex than some others. The first layer especially requires fast manipulation to get everything done before the water glaze dries.

MATERIALS LIST

Sample board coated with low-luster creamy yellow oil paint, B.M. (Benjamin Moore) 180 or similar

Two No. 2 oval sash brushes for glaze application

Palette and/or containers for glazes

Water glaze: one part Cassel Brown to one part Raw Sienna

Oil glaze: one part Cassel Brown to one part Raw Sienna

Small and medium spalters

Badger blender

No. 8 fan brush or veinette and comb

Oil-blending brush

Plastic wrap

Spray shellac (optional)

Fine-grade synthetic scrubbing pad (optional)

Whiting

Paint thinner for cleanup

1 | The base color for bird's-eye maple is a very light creamy yellow; B.M. 180 works well. Brush on the water glaze and quickly lay it out with a medium spalter. Be sure to finish laying out in the direction of the grain.

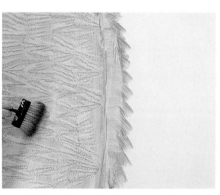

2 | Wipe off the spalter, then holding the bristles in a curved grip, walk the spalter down the surface to create the broad moiré pattern. If you can't finish the panel all at once, be sure to leave a "wet edge" so you can pick up the texture and marry the sections together.

3 | Soften the moirés by moving the badger blender in a side-to-side motion.

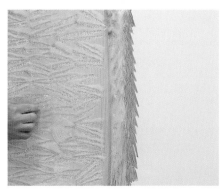

4 | Moisten a finger and touch the surface to create the "eyes." Group them in threes and twos and a few singles.

5 | Soften the eyes in one diagonal direction only.

6 │ When the surface has dried, you have the option of fixing this layer with a coat of spray shellac. This is not absolutely necessary, but since you will be using a water glaze to draw on the next layer of grain, a mistake could mean having to wipe off the whole panel and start over. If you seal the surface now, the mistake can be wiped off without disturbing the first glaze.

7 │ If you seal the surface with shellac, you will have to deglaze the surface after it has dried or the next water glaze will bead up. You can do this by rubbing the surface lightly with a fine-grade synthetic scrubbing pad. Be careful not to rub through the shellac.

8 │ While it is also possible to draw in the heart grain with a small brush, this technique uses only straight grain. Use a fan brush or veinette to lay in a series of fine parallel lines using the same water glaze you used for the moirés. Try to make these lines in one continuous stroke, reloading the brush before beginning each pass. See page 37 for a detailed explanation of this technique.

9 │ Apply the oil glaze (left), then use a small spalter (right) to lay out the glaze and, as always, finish up in the direction of the grain.

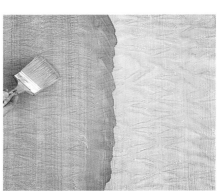

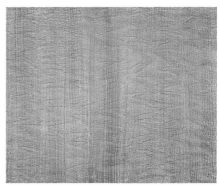

10 │ Press a piece of pleated plastic food wrap into the wet oil glaze to create rows of subtle horizontal moirés.

11 │ Soften the moirés with an oil-blending brush.

12 │ Add the oil glaze to the rest of the panel and work into the wet edge to marry the two parts together. Repeat the steps on the second half to complete the panel.

CREATING SATINWOOD

Satinwood has a very complex system of moirés that seems to shimmer as the light strikes it from different angles, hence its name. It has been used to veneer furniture in many styles and periods. I prefer to do this finish entirely using water glazes in order to get as close as possible to the subtlety of the actual wood. I used B.M. 194 for the base coat for this sample, but a slightly lighter base coat would work well also.

MATERIALS LIST

Sample board coated with B.M. (Benjamin Moore) 194 or similar

Palette and/or containers for glazes

Water glaze: four parts Raw Sienna to two parts Yellow Ochre to one part Cassel Earth

Brush for glaze application

Medium spalter for water glaze

Large, round sash or house-painters' brush

Flogger

Badger blender

Thin plastic shopping bags

Varnish and brush or shellac (if desired)

Torn cardboard comb

Whiting

Paint thinner for cleanup

1 | Begin with the B.M. 194 alkyd base color. Then brush on and lay out with a medium spalter a water glaze of four parts Raw Sienna, two parts Yellow Ochre and one part Cassel Earth.

2 | Immediately stroke through the glaze with a torn cardboard comb to create the fine linear straight grain. Maintain a parallel direction with these strokes.

3 | Lightly flog the board to suggest some of the underlying pore structure. Be careful not to hit the board so heavily that you destroy the lines.

4 | Use the badger blender in the direction of the grain to lightly soften.

5 | Lightly roll a large round housepainters' brush through the wet glaze in the direction of the grain to suggest the underlying grain.

6 | Let this layer dry and seal with a coat of shellac or varnish.

7 | When dry, deglaze by dusting with whiting and brush on a second layer of the same water glaze. Then use the spalter to create a pattern of moirés on the board.

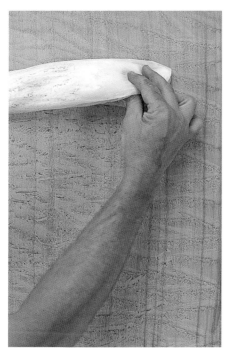

8 | For this step, prepare a tool ahead of time by putting one thin plastic shopping bag inside another and forming them into a sausage shape. Roll this tool up the board to create a series of linear disruptions in the moirés.

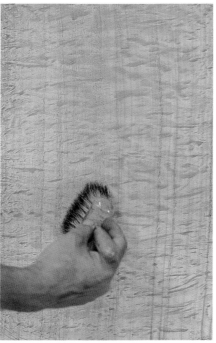

9 | Soften again with the badger brush but this time move it horizontally across the board to stretch out the broken moirés.

10 | When the board is dry, varnish it for the finished sample.

CREATING CROTCH MAHOGANY

Crotch mahogany, also referred to as flame or feather, is cut from the tree where branches split off from the main trunk. The figuring is caused by this split and from the intergrowth that occurs around it. The wood is always used as a veneer and is commonly book-matched (two pieces are placed next to each other in a mirror image configuration). The wet-in-wet water glaze technique you will use to create the figure requires relative quickness and a practiced feel for the form. The good thing is that since it is a water glaze you can wipe it off and start over if it looks awkward.

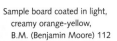

MATERIALS LIST

Sample board coated in light, creamy orange-yellow, B.M. (Benjamin Moore) 112

Palettes and/or containers for glazes

Water glazes
• Glaze No. 1: eight parts Alizarin Crimson to four parts Burnt Umber to one part Mars Black
• Glaze No. 2: two parts Burnt Umber to one part Mars Black

Oil glaze: two parts Cassel Earth to one part Alizarin Crimson

Two No. 2 oval sash brushes for glaze

¾" round pointed housepainters' brush

Worn or shredded sea sponge

Small, medium and large spalters

Badger blender and cod-tail oil blender

Veinette or similar brush and comb

Tooth spalter

Varnish and brush

Paint thinner for cleanup

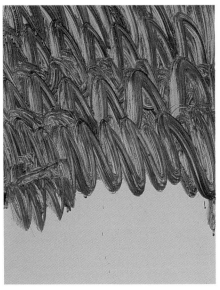

1 | Begin with the sample board base coated with B.M. 112, then brush on the water glaze of eight parts Alizarin Crimson, four parts Burnt Umber and one part Mars Black. Use a medium spalter to lay out the glaze. Practice doing this until you can accomplish the operation quickly.

2 | Use the darker water glaze of two parts Burnt Umber to one part Mars Black and a ¾" round pointed housepainters' brush to draw a sort of plant or stalk formation into the wet red glaze. This figure should have a little tilt to it and be slightly off center. Practice this step on a dry board until you feel comfortable with the process.

3 | Immediately soften this figure with the badger blender and a side-to-side motion.

4 | Use a worn or shredded sea sponge to draw the grain lines into the wet glaze. Starting with light pressure in the stalk and increasing the pressure as you move out from the center, draw the grain out and down in a sweeping arc. As you move away from the stalk, the lines should become more parallel to the stalk.

5 | Soften with the badger blender, this time from the center out toward the edge.

6 | Use a wet veinette that has been combed (to separate the bristles) to connect the grain lines in the middle of the figure. Let dry.

7 | Apply the oil glaze of two parts Cassel Earth and one part Alizarin Crimson to the entire board, and lay out with a large spalter.

8 | With a tooth spalter and some of the same oil glaze, add additional dark lines next to the thin ones you drew with the veinette in the middle of the figure.

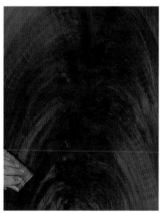

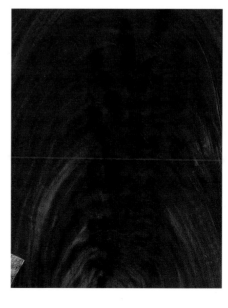

9 | Following the existing grain lines, create moirés in the grain pattern using both large and small spalters.

10 | Soften the moirés with the badger or cod-tail blending brush.

11 | Let dry thoroughly and varnish.

CREATING ELM BURL WOOD

Burl wood is cut from lumpy growths on trees, and exhibits many small knots and twisted grain patterns. The burls themselves are not very large, so the veneers cut from them are usually no bigger than 12" × 18". There are many types of burls, but if you learn the basic techniques shown here, you'll be able to adapt them for most other types.

Burl veneers are often used in bookmatch configuration or applied in such a way that the grain pattern repeats in a predictable way. When you use the burl wood this way, you will find it helpful to make a drawing to work from so you can repeat the relationship of knots and grain and maintain the proper direction. If you plan to make a book-match, make a two-sided drawing by holding it up to a window and repeating your sketch on the back. This way you can flip it over for the book-match, which is just what happens when the real wood is used.

MATERIALS LIST

Sample board coated with B.M. (Benjamin Moore) 124

Palettes and/or containers for glazes

Water glazes
- Glaze No. 1: one part Burnt Sienna to one part Burnt Umber
- Glaze No. 2: Cassel Earth or one part Burnt Umber to one part Mars Black

Oil glaze: one part Burnt Umber to one part Burnt Sienna

Medium spalter for water glaze

Small and medium spalters

Three brushes for glaze application

Stencil brush (optional)

Veinette or similar brush and comb

No. 2 pointed watercolor brush

Badger blender

Worn or shredded sea sponge

Bristle blender (optional)

Torn cardboard for moirés (optional)

Paint thinner for cleanup

1 | Begin with a base coat of B.M. 124, a slightly orangish straw color. Then brush on a water glaze of one part Burnt Sienna to one part Burnt Umber.

2 | Lay out the glaze with a medium spalter to create a bit of movement to the glaze. This will establish the direction of the grain in the burl.

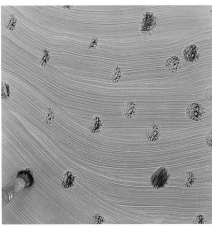

3 | With another glaze brush or a stencil brush, touch in spots of the darker water glaze of either Cassel Earth or four parts Burnt Umber to one part black. Make the spots of color irregular in size and placement, grouping some spots close together and others farther apart.

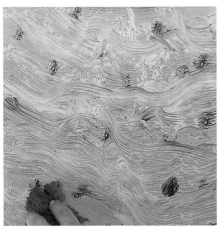

4 | While the surface is still wet, use a damp sea sponge to texture the surface around and between the knots. Try both rolling and dragging the sponge in the direction of the initial spalted glaze.

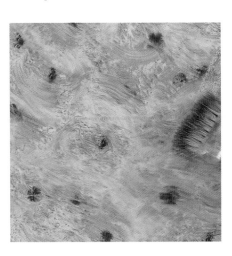

5 | Immediately soften the surface with a badger blender. If the knots lose their shape, they can be redefined with a small pointed brush and some of the darker glaze. Let dry.

6 | With the veinette combed to open up the bristles, use the first water glaze plus some additional liquid to lay in a series of fine lines following the general direction of the sponge marks, but work around the knots. Let dry.

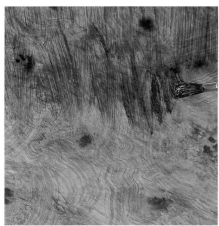

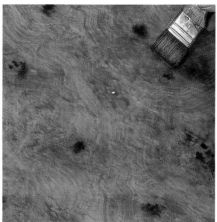

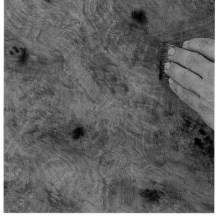

7 | Apply the oil glaze of one part Burnt Umber to one part Burnt Sienna, and even it out with a small spalter.

8 | Use the small spalter to create a series of moirés around the knots. A piece of torn cardboard can also be used for this step, especially if the glaze has begun to thicken while you are working.

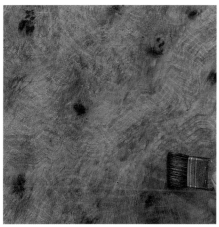

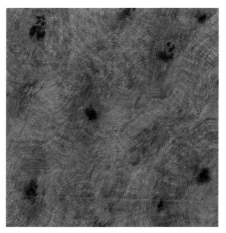

9 | Use a spalter or blending brush to soften the moirés.

10 | When the oil glaze has dried thoroughly apply a coat of varnish to enhance and protect the panted finish.

CREATING WALNUT

Like mahogany, walnut graining requires you to draw the heart grain. While both woods share the same overall relationship of a series of ever extending Vs, the walnut heart-grain pattern is more jagged and irregular then the mahogany.

MATERIALS LIST

Sample board coated with B.M. (Benjamin Moore) 194

Palette and/or containers for glazes

Water glazes
• Glaze No. 1: Burnt Umber
• Glaze No. 2: Cassel Earth
• Glaze No. 3: one part Burnt Sienna to one part Burnt Umber

Oil glazes
• Glaze No. 1: Burnt Umber
• Glaze No. 2: one part Burnt Umber to one part Burnt Sienna

Brushes for glaze application

Artists' oil paints: Mars Black, Prussian Blue

Flogger

Tooth spalter

Pencil over-grainer

Small and medium spalters

No. 6 hog-bristle filbert

Badger blender

Whiting

Tapes: painters', drafting and ⅛" automotive

Spray shellac (optional)

Paint thinner for cleanup

1 | On a base coat of B.M. 194, using a separate glaze brush for each, lay on alternating stripes of water glaze No. 1, Burnt Umber, and No. 2, Cassel Earth.

2 | Stretch out the glazes with a medium spalter, and immediately flog to create the underlying pore structure. Let dry.

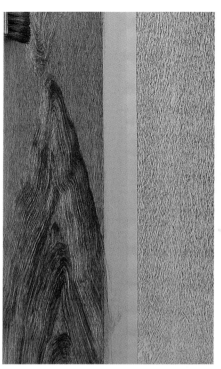

3 | Tape off a section of the sample board to mimic a board, then with an oil glaze brush, lay on the No. 1 oil glaze of Burnt Umber, and stretch it out with a small spalter.

4 | Give the glaze a few moments to set up and then, using the tooth spalter and the No. 2 oil glaze of Burnt Umber and Burnt Sienna, begin sketching in the grain pattern.

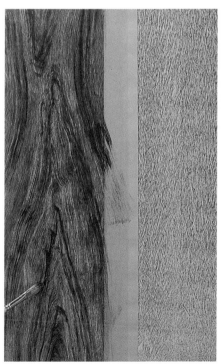

5 | With the pencil over-grainer and oil glaze No. 2, begin to strengthen the heart-grain figure. As you do so, pick up dabs of the other palette colors to add variety to the coloration.

6 | Use the No. 6 filbert and oil glaze No. 2 along with palette colors to further refine the grain structure.

7 | Use the small spalter to soften from the center out, and let the oil glaze dry overnight.

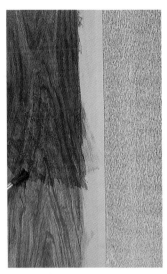

9 | Brush on the No. 3 water overglaze of Burnt Sienna and Burnt Umber, and stretch it out with the medium spalter. Add moirés.

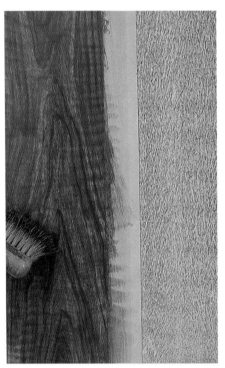

8 | When the surface is dry to the touch, dust it with whiting so it will accept the water overglaze.

10 | Soften with the badger blender and let dry.

11 | While covering the rest of your sample, lightly coat the finished part with spray shellac. This step is optional; it will protect your first board from an accidental splatter as you continue to work.

12 | Develop the grain pattern on the rest of the sample, but vary this part by showing more straight grain. The tools and steps are the same but only a few small Vs are introduced at the left side of the board. Since the first board is still rather fresh, remove the tape as soon as you have finished the oil glaze. Then let it dry.

13 | Apply a fresh piece of tape and dust with whiting. Then brush on the water overglaze, texture it and let it dry.

14 | Varnish the overglaze and remove the tape for the finished sample.

CREATING AMBOYNA BURL

For amboyna burl you will need the same color sample board, oil glaze and water glazes as for the elm burl. You will also need the same tools with the exception of the veinette, stencil brush and cardboard moiré tool.

MATERIALS LIST

Sample board coated with B.M. (Benjamin Moore) 124

Palette and/or containers for glazes

Water glazes
• Glaze No. 1: one part Burnt Sienna to one part Burnt Umber
• Glaze No. 2: Cassel Earth or one part Burnt Umber to one part Mars Black

Oil Glaze: Burnt Umber

Small and medium spalters

Three brushes for glaze application

No. 2 pointed watercolor brush

Badger blender

Worn or shredded sea sponge

Large spalter or bristle blender

Paper towels with a bumpy texture

Varnish and brush

Paint thinner for cleanup

1 Use the same B.M. 124 base color and No. 1 water glaze for the amboyna burl as for the elm burl, but lay out the glaze evenly over the panel.

2 With a different brush, touch in spots of the darker No. 2 water glaze randomly on the panel grouping some spots closer than others.

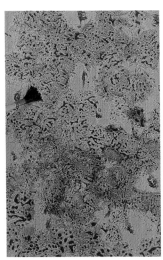

3 Returning to the original brush, vigorously stipple the water glaze so that it begins to pull up into amoeba-shaped droplets. Work around the darker areas and then do them last to avoid their being over-shadowed by the more predominant glaze. If the dark areas are lost in the overall effect, you can lay in some more of the darker glaze and continue to stipple.

4 While the glaze is wet, use the sea sponge rolled lightly through the glaze to vary the density of the stippled surface.

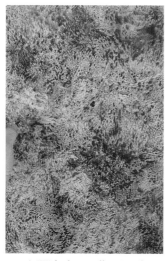

5 | Immediately take up the badger blender and lightly soften the surface. Some areas should be only slightly whisked once while others can show a little smudging from the blending. Soften in a variety of directions so the shapes retain a round rather than oblong shape, which would be the case if you soften in one direction only.

6 | With the small pointed watercolor brush, add some individual dark spots for emphasis and to balance the composition. Let dry.

7 | Use the oil glaze brush to apply the Burnt Umber overglaze, and stretch it out with the small spalter.

8 | Crumple a paper towel and press it into the wet oil glaze to remove some of the glaze and open up areas of the base color. Keep changing the surface of the towel so that you don't reapply the glaze.

9 | Use the bristle softener or large spalter to soften the overall effect.

10 | The finished panel exhibits the characteristic multitude "eyes" of this unusual wood. When the sample dries, varnish it to protect and enhance the finish.

CREATING WEATHERED PINE

This technique exhibits the characteristics of a sample of wood that has twisted as it has grown. The streaks and spots suggest infestation or exposure and discoloration while growing or after being cut into boards. It produces a more rustic appearance than some other techniques, one that has a lively and convincing grain pattern especially suitable for simpler pieces of furniture. This sample shows how several boards are assembled to form a diagonal panel with a frame.

MATERIALS LIST

Sample board coated with a light straw color, B.M. (Benjamin Moore) 1110

Oil glaze: three parts Raw Sienna to one part Burnt Umber

Artists' oil paints: Mars Black, Burnt Sienna, Cassel Earth and Burnt Umber

Palette and/or containers for glazes

Water glazes
• Glaze No. 1: two parts Raw Sienna to one part Burnt Umber
• Glaze No. 2: two parts Raw Sienna to one part Burnt Umber to one part Kremer Translucent Red, #52400

Small can of oil glaze medium

No. 2 oval sash brushes for glaze application

Small and medium spalters

Cotton swabs

Burlap

Cheesecloth

Varnish and brush

Painters' tape in two widths

Spattering brush

Whiting

Paint thinner for cleanup

1 | This diagram, drawn with blue tape, shows you how to construct a diagonal panel with border that would be appropriate for building a simple piece of furniture such as the blanket chest project. Don't confuse these taped lines with those that are used elsewhere to create inlay. I have used the thin blue tape lines here just for visibility. The lines would normally be drawn with a pencil.

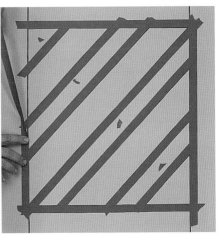

2 | After drawing your design on the board, tape off the frame and alternate diagonal boards with painters' tape. Marking the boards will help avoid the confusion of which boards are being taped off and which are being painted.

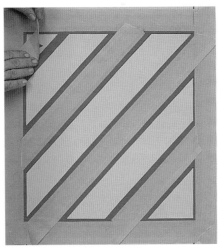

3 | Finish protecting the masked off areas with wider tape.

4 | Get your palette ready with the following artists' oil colors: Burnt Umber, Burnt Sienna, Cassel Earth and Mars Black. Mix the main oil glaze of three parts Raw Sienna to one part Burnt Umber in a plastic tray and keep it separate from the other colors.

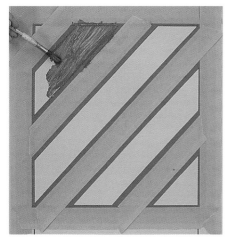

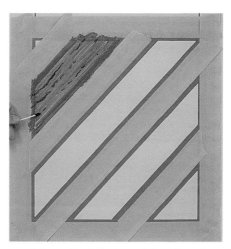

5 | Use a glaze brush to apply the main oil glaze to a section of the design.

6 | Immediately begin applying bits and streaks of the different color oil paints, mixed with a little glaze medium into the wet glaze. You can use small brushes for this operation, but cotton swabs work well and they can be discarded if they dry out.

7 | Use a small spalter to lightly blend the small bits of color.

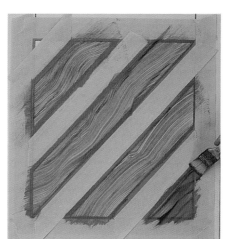

8 | Draw a folded piece of burlap through the wet glaze, twisting and turning it randomly to simulate changes in the direction of the grain.

9 | Continue this process until all the exposed sections have been glazed and textured. You will need to refold the burlap as it becomes clogged with paint. Let dry overnight or longer depending on the glaze medium you have used.

10 | Dust the surface with whiting to prepare it for the water overglaze. Brush off any excess whiting.

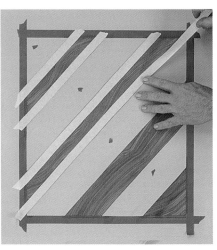

11 Brush on the water glaze of two parts Raw Sienna to one part Burnt Umber, lay it out with a spalter, then wipe through it with a piece of folded cheesecloth, removing most of the glaze but leaving a series of fine lines. Let dry, then varnish.

12 Remove the tape from the unpainted sections, and tape off the finished sections.

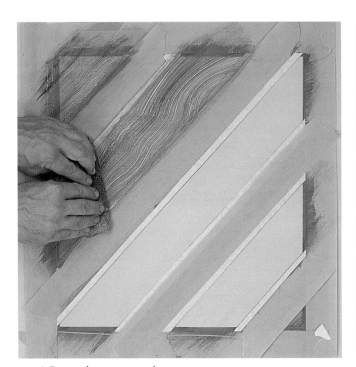

13 Repeat the process on the exposed sections.

14 After all the sections have been grained and varnished, remove all the tape to reveal the completed panel.

15 | Tape off the central panel, and grain and varnish the top and bottom borders using water glaze No. 2 for a slightly deeper color effect.

16 | Grain the side borders and remove all the tape.

17 | Here is the finished panel. Apply additional coats of varnish for more protection and a finer finish.

CREATING HEART-GRAIN MAHOGANY

Mahogany is a rich, dark tropical wood used extensively in furniture making. The heart grain is composed of a series of gently rounded Vs that often have a little dip in the end of the V. It can vary in color from orange-brown to deep crimson. For this rather deep red version, start your sample with a base coat of B.M. 1194. Remember to deglaze the surface of your sample board before you start.

MATERIALS LIST

Sample board coated with B.M. (Benjamin Moore) 1194

Palette and/or containers for glazes

Water glazes
- Glaze No. 1: two parts Burnt Umber to one part Mars Black
- Glaze No. 2: two parts Alizarin Crimson to one part Cassel Earth

Oil glaze: two parts Burnt Umber to one part Burnt Sienna to one part Alizarin Crimson

Three No. 2 oval sash brushes for glaze application

Small and medium spalters

Flogger

Tooth spalter

Pointed, large squirrel-hair brush (cat's tongue)

Bristle blender (cod tail)

Badger blender

No. 6 hog bristle filbert

Burlap

Cheesecloth

Whiting

Drafting tape

Varnish and brush

Paint thinner for cleanup

1 | To create the pore structure, begin by brushing on a coat of water glaze made from two parts Burnt Umber to one part Mars Black.

2 | Use a medium spalter to lay out the glaze. Brush across the glaze first, then in the direction of the grain.

3 | Starting at the near end of the board and moving away from yourself, use the flogging brush to strike the surface to create the underlying pore structure. Be sure to keep the rows of marks parallel to each other as you move across the board.

4 | After the water glaze has dried, tape off a section of the sample to create one board. Then brush on an oil glaze of two parts Burnt Umber and one part each of Burnt Sienna and Alizarin Crimson.

5 | Lay out the oil glaze with a small spalter in the direction of the grain.

6 | While the glaze is fresh, use a tooth spalter to draw in the main V-shape grain pattern. You can work to create the Vs in one direction only, or you can show the V-shapes reversing direction within the board (as shown here). Maintain the brush in the same position relative to the pattern of the grain as you create the Vs.

7 | Use a small piece of folded burlap to create the straight-grain pattern at the sides of the Vs.

8 | Use a folded piece of cheesecloth stretched over your thumb to wipe out some more distinctive lines within the Vs.

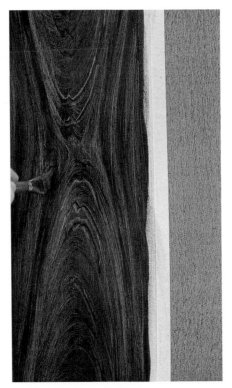

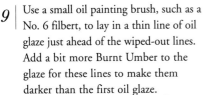

9 | Use a small oil painting brush, such as a No. 6 filbert, to lay in a thin line of oil glaze just ahead of the wiped-out lines. Add a bit more Burnt Umber to the glaze for these lines to make them darker than the first oil glaze.

10 | Use a soft-bristled, pointed brush, called a cat's tongue, to lay in some darker lines in the straight-grain sections of the board. You can use the same color glaze used for the darker accent lines in the Vs. If you add a little more of the oil glaze medium, it will help the glaze flow off the brush.

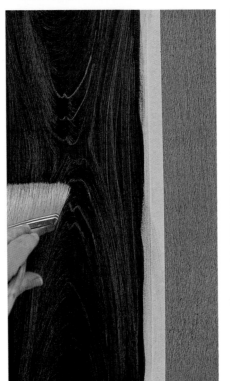

11 | Use a bristle softener to lightly pull the colors together. Soften mahogany by starting at the center and working out.

12 | Allow the oil glaze to dry thoroughly, then brush on or dust the surface with whiting. Do not scrub as you would to deglaze an oil surface when first starting a water glaze application. Doing so will erode the oil glaze.

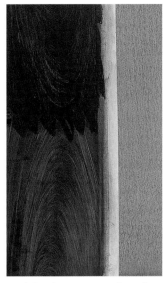

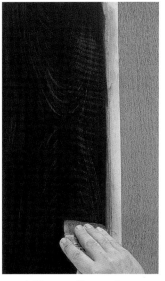

13 | Brush on a water glaze of two parts Alizarin Crimson to one part Cassel Earth.

14 | Use a medium spalter to lay out the glaze. With the same brush, add some moirés at a slight angle to the direction of the grain.

15 | Soften the water glaze by barely touching the surface with a badger softener.

16 | Varnish this section of the sample, then when dry, tape it off and proceed to the next board.

17 | The complete varnished sample consisting of the two boards.

CREATING ZEBRAWOOD

This wood is similar in pattern and execution to Macassar ebony. However, it does have some darker diagonal grain that must be laid in with a script liner or similar pointed brush.

MATERIALS LIST

Sample board coated with B.M. (Benjamin Moore) 234 or similar

Palette and/or containers for glazes

Water glazes
- Glaze No. 1: four parts Burnt Umber to one part Mars Black
- Glaze No. 2: two parts Burnt Umber and one part Mars Black
- Glaze No. 3: Burnt Umber

Oil glaze: Burnt Umber

Two No. 2 oval sash brushes for glaze application

Small and medium spalters

Badger blender

No. 1 script liner

Toothbrush for spattering

Torn and cut cardboard comb

Fine-grade synthetic scrubbing pad

Craft stick

Varnish and brush

Paint thinner for cleanup

1 On a base coat of B.M. 234 Satin Impervo, lay on a water glaze of four parts Burnt Umber to one part Mars Black. As with all water glazes, work quickly to give yourself time for manipulation before the glaze begins to set up.

2 Use a medium spalter to lay out the water glaze. Work across, and then with, the direction of the grain to achieve a uniform distribution.

3 Pull a cut and torn cardboard comb through the glaze to create the parallel straight grain. Each stroke should be continuous without stops or hesitations. Make sure the lines don't cross over each other or run at odd angles.

4 Immediately soften the straight-grain pattern with a badger blender. Use long strokes at a very slight angle to the direction of the grain.

5 | With another water glaze mixed from two parts Burnt Umber and one part Mars Black, lay in some diagonal grain lines with a script liner. These lines should run only slightly angular to the straight-grain and should branch off of and connect to some of the previous straight grain lines.

6 | Use a toothbrush and craft stick to speckle the pore structure with a third water glaze of Burnt Umber.

7 | With the badger blender, soften the specks in the direction of the grain to elongate them.

8 | Apply an oil glaze of Burnt Umber, and lay out with a small spalter.

9 | With light pressure, pull a fine scrubbing pad through the Burnt Umber glaze. This will lighten the overall effect and create a fine linear pattern in the glaze. Again, make sure the strokes cover the entire area and are continuous. You may repeat this procedure to further lighten the final tonality.

10 | Varnish when dry to complete the sample.

COUNTRY-GRAINING SAMPLES

Country graining results in colorful and energetic patterns that are loose interpretations of woodgrain. Lacking expensive tools and hard-to-find materials, self-taught country grainers used locally available products to carry out their decorative work. This technique was often referred to as "putty" painting or "vinegar" painting due to the use of these materials. Putty was frequently used as a texturing tool, and vinegar was used as the liquid vehicle for the paint.

The paint I use for country graining is the same vinegar, pigment and detergent formula described in chapter two as a "water" glaze. Mix ⅛ teaspoon dish detergent to a pint of apple-cider vinegar for the medium. Then mix this medium with dry pigment at a ratio of two parts medium to one part pigment. You may have to adjust the ratio of medium from pigment to pigment as each has slightly different mixing characteristics. Since this is reversible or impermanent medium, you will need to varnish all your samples after they dry.

MATERIALS LIST

Sample boards coated with French Yellow Ochre or similar color oil or latex/acrylic enamel (I used Muralo Ultra brand acrylic paint with an eggshell finish which Muralo calls "Pigskin.")

Palette and/or containers for glazes

Vinegar glazes
• Burnt Umber
• Burnt Sienna
• Prussian Blue

Three No. 2 oval sash brushes for glaze application

Vinyl glazing compound or putty

2" foam brush

Feather

Varnish and brush

Paint thinner for cleanup

1 | Roll a small lump of vinyl glazing compound into a finger shape for this technique.

2 | Brush on a fairly heavy coat of the Burnt Sienna glaze. If it beads up, try using a scrubbing action with the brush.

3 | Press the glazing compound into the wet glaze so that the marks overlap slightly. Here, I have created rows of the finger-shaped marks. Since the material is soft, it changes slightly with each mark, giving the work an organic quality.

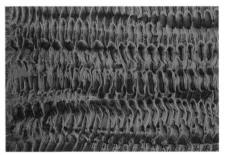

4 | The finished panel has a woodgrain character, but is somewhat stylized. The strong base color also lends a strong color effect.

You can achieve similar results using a feather pressed into the paint. Here again, I have created a series of marks in rows, but you can move the feather in an arc or curve.

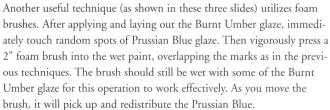

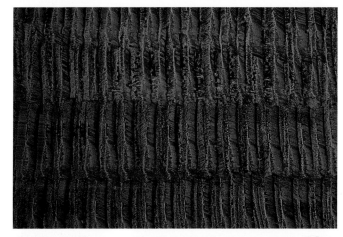

Another useful technique (as shown in these three slides) utilizes foam brushes. After applying and laying out the Burnt Umber glaze, immediately touch random spots of Prussian Blue glaze. Then vigorously press a 2" foam brush into the wet paint, overlapping the marks as in the previous techniques. The brush should still be wet with some of the Burnt Umber glaze for this operation to work effectively. As you move the brush, it will pick up and redistribute the Prussian Blue.

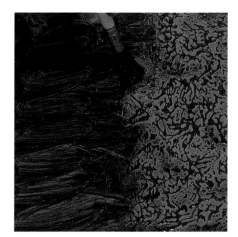

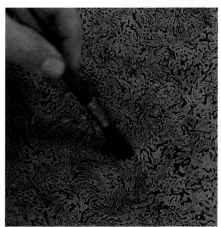

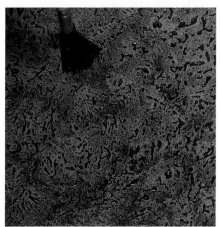

For a burl-like effect, first coat the sample board with Burnt Umber glaze and immediately proceed using the same brush with a very active stippling action. This should cause the paint to bubble up as you whip air into it. As the small bubbles break, the paint will settle into amoeba-like shapes, suggesting burl wood. Then dab in small spots of Prussian Blue just as was done in the last sample, and stipple the surface again to redistribute the spots. The result is this burl-type finish, a subtle greenish color variation. Be sure to varnish all of your samples after they dry.

step-by-step projects

Working with furniture will be more enjoyable and successful if you consider in advance the structural relationships between the parts and how these can aid or inhibit a convincing and aesthetic graining result.

Develop a good visual inventory of how furniture looks. Go to museums and antique shops to study how real woods are combined in furniture construction. Collect photos of furniture with interesting grain patterns from magazines. Purchase a few books on high-quality collectible and antique furniture for reference.

You can use graining techniques with furniture in two basic ways. One way is to suggest that the object is constructed from a particular type of wood. If your grain pattern is to look structural — that is, to create the illusion of solid wood construction — it should run in the direction of the long dimension in any part, such as legs or drawer fronts. For convincing effects, apply the grain pattern/color to all edges, inside corners and other places where it would normally show.

The other way to use graining techniques is to suggest that veneers have been applied to the surface.

The grain of painted veneers can run in any direction, and this is commonly used for decorative effect. When veneers are applied to create a simple geometric detail, it's called inlay. When veneers are applied to create a complex design, whether geometric or pictorial, it is referred to as marquetry.

Before you begin a project, consider its pros and cons. Choose to paint furniture that has flat surfaces and little detail and that is made of hard, close-grained woods such as maple. Avoid pieces that have raised edges, carvings or hard-to-reach areas, such as shelves, which will make your job more difficult.

If the piece has doors, consider whether you will also need to grain the back sides. If the interior will be visible, either because the doors have glass or because they will be open for display, you will need to finish it to complement the exterior.

Remember that parts will be easier to paint if you can separate them from the main body of the piece. This, of course, applies to doors and table leaves, but also check to see if legs, tabletops, etc., are screwed or bolted on. If they can be removed without damaging the piece (even if this means prying off a glue block), do so and paint them separately.

mahogany writing table

This delicate writing table painted as heart-grain mahogany is at home in the guest room or in a quiet reading space in any room of the house. By using an ebony black finish on the Queen Anne legs, you not only emphasize this graceful element of the table, but also avoid the difficult task of attempting to grain their round curving surfaces.

1 | Begin by base coating with B.M. 1194 or a similar color. Then lay out the top to allow for mitered ends. Tape off the mitered sections, then create the pore structure by applying and flogging the water glaze of two parts Burnt Umber to one part Mars Black.

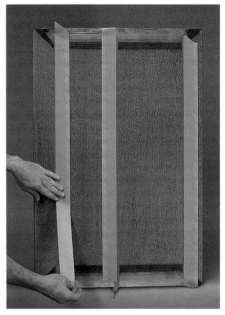

2 | After the water glaze dries, create the four boards within the top by taping off alternate sections. Use 2"-wide painters' tape to back up the ¾" painters' masking tape for a margin of safety. The edge boards are mitered to match up with the ends.

3 | Apply the oil glaze of two parts Burnt Umber, one part Burnt Sienna and one part Alizarin Crimson.

4 | Manipulate the oil glaze as shown in the previous chapters, and soften with the bristle softener.

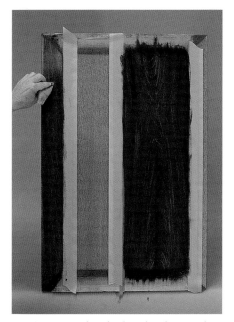

5 | Move to the edge board and repeat the process. Let these two boards dry.

6 | Dust the panels with whiting, and apply the water overglaze made up of two parts Alizarin Crimson and one part Cassel Earth.

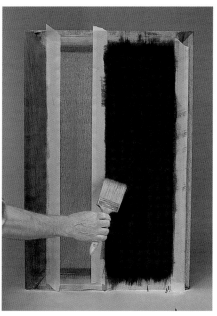

7 | Brush out this glaze and manipulate to create the moirés and to soften.

8 | Varnish these two sections before moving on.

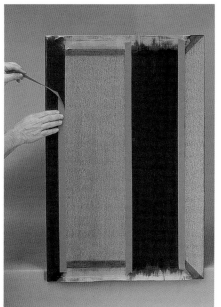

9 | Remove the tapes that created the edges of these boards, and apply new tape to isolate the remaining two boards.

10 | Apply and manipulate the oil glaze on these sections. Try for a similar, though not exactly matching, pattern.

13 | While the top is drying, begin work on the table apron. Use the same basic techniques to grain each of the four sides.

11 | When the oil glaze dries, dust on a layer of whiting. If you are working vertically, you can accomplish this by wrapping the whiting up in a piece of cheesecloth and tapping the surface. Brush off any excess with a softening brush.

12 | Apply the water and oil glazes to the two end boards and varnish.

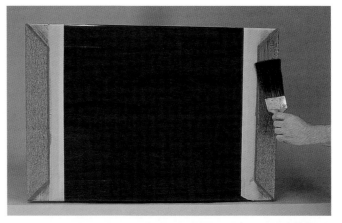

15 | Apply the water and oil glazes to these two end boards and varnish.

14 | After the top has dried, remove all the tape, and tape off the two end mitered boards.

16 | Remove the tape and varnish the entire top. Keep in mind that a light sanding is recommended after the second and subsequent coats of varnish.

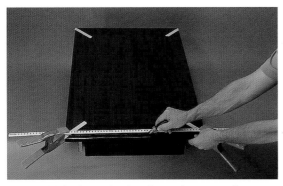

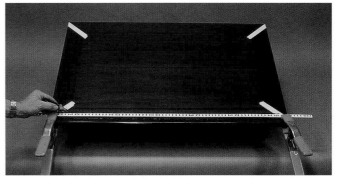

17 | Add the linear detail to the top by using a thin, straightedge held in place with two spring clamps as a guide for the lining tool. Place tape along the miter lines to provide start and end stops. Then fill the lining tool with black latex enamel and pull it along both sides of the straightedge to create the appearance of a double line of ebony inlay.

18 | After you line both ends of the tabletop, remove the start/stop tapes and reposition them so you can line the other two edges.

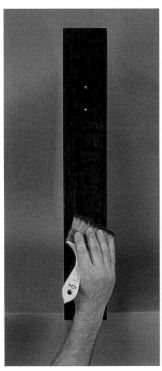

20 | Don't forget to do the ends of the drawer.

21 | Prime and paint the legs with black satin finish oil enamel to simulate ebony.

19 | Grain the drawer using the same techniques.

22 | Assemble the table and apply the hardware to complete the project.

satinwood end table

This low table has the convenience of two drawers, and though it's a small piece, its bulk gives it an imposing stature. The satinwood finish counteracts its boxy lines to lend a lighter, more elegant quality. Taped lines, simulating light wood inlay, and black painted lines, suggesting ebony inlay, create an engaging emphasis to the pattern of the veneer. By being careful when sealing the water glazes, you can minimize the use of protective taping. If you find this procedure difficult, you can use wider tapes to protect the alternate diamonds on the top.

Primer

B.M. (Benjamin Moore) 194 or similar for base coat

Palette and/or containers for glazes

Water glaze: four parts Raw Sienna to two parts Yellow Ochre to one part Cassel Earth

Black latex enamel

Varnish and brush

Whiting

Brushes for primer and base coat

Brush for glaze application

Medium spalter

Large, round sash or house-painters' brush

Flogger

Badger blender

Sandpaper

Drawing tools: straightedge, ruler and pencil

Tapes: painters', drafting and ⅛" automotive

Lining tool

Thin plastic shopping bags

Fine-grade synthetic scrubbing pads

Spray shellac

Paint thinner for cleanup

1 | This two-drawer end table has a sturdy form. With a satin-wood finish and some decorative line work, you can give it a new feeling of elegance.

2 | After priming and base coating, begin by using ⅛" masking tape to establish a 1½" border on the top. Create the crisscross pattern by taping an X from corner to corner, then make one large diamond using the midpoints of the sides as the points of the diamond. Follow this simple procedure, and you will only have to measure the midpoints of the four sides to create all the diamonds.

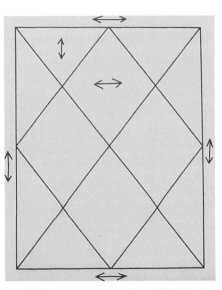

3 | Use tape to temporarily establish the direction of the grain on the diamond pattern. Since you will be changing the direction on every other diamond, it is important that you avoid confusion. Also, the pattern will look best if the graining on the borders and the half diamonds next to them run in different directions.

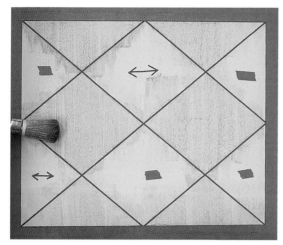

4 | With the alternate sections marked with tape, in the unmarked sections, begin laying on and texturing the first layer of water glaze made up of four parts Raw Sienna, two parts Yellow Ochre, one part Cassel Earth. Proceed just as you would on a sample board, doing all sections at the same time. The only difference is that you don't need to put any water glaze on the marked-off sections.

5 | Varnish (shellac can be used as a sealer only if you plan to finish with alkyd varnish) these sections after they dry, then wipe off the glaze that was left in the other diamonds.

6 | Apply and texture the remaining diamond sections, but establish the grain direction at a right angle to the first group.

7 | Once again, seal the newly grained sections, then wipe off any extra glaze that was deposited on the alternate diamonds.

8 | Deglaze the entire surface with a light rubbing of a fine-grade abrasive pad.

11 | Remove the wide tapes from the borders and reposition them to protect the top. Texture the borders with the grain running in the long direction. Complete two opposing sides of the border, then remove and reposition the corner tapes and finish the other two sides.

9 | Following the same general procedures, apply and texture the second layer of the same water glaze layer over the first, using the tools and techniques demonstrated on the sample board.

10 | Texture and seal the second set of diamonds to complete the graining of this part of the top.

12 | To give extra detail to the design, use the lining tool and black latex paint to replicate the border and diamond pattern. Apply ¼" drafting tape to provide the correct spacing for the diamonds, then draw four long lines to begin to create the individual diamond shapes.

13 | Change the placement of the tapes, and draw four long lines in the other direction to finish the diamonds.

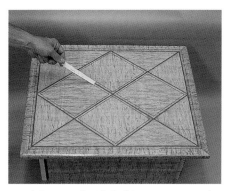

14 | Remove the ¼" drafting tapes to reveal the spaces between the black diamond lines.

15 | Remove the ⅛" masking tape to expose the base color, which appears as an inlay of light wood. Add two additional coats of varnish to protect the line work and give a high-quality finish.

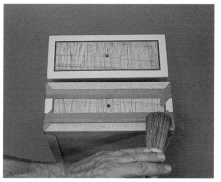

16 | While waiting for the varnish to dry on the top, begin working on the drawers. Tape off borders and grain them in the long direction. Use the same techniques as on the top.

17 | Since the legs can be detached, you can lay them down to work on them. By positioning them close together, you can grain one side of all four at once. Just be careful that your sealer between glazes doesn't run down the sides. Use spray shellac to eliminate that possibility.

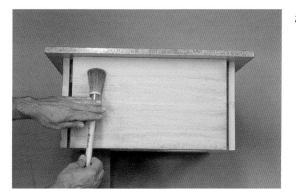

18 | As the other parts are drying, grain the sides and varnish them.

19 | When all the parts have been grained, lined and varnished, reassemble the table and replace the hardware to complete the project.

crotch mahogany chest of drawers

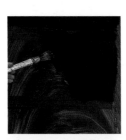

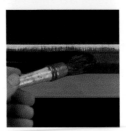

This small chest of drawers is ideal for graining with the crotch mahogany finish. It is not so big that it's overbearing, and its plain surface allows you to manipulate the glazes easily. Book-match the front and top, and paint a single crotch on the end panels. The overlap technique used on the drawers allows you to create an inlay line in a simple yet convincing manner.

MATERIALS LIST

Primer

Palette and/or containers for glazes

B.M. (Benjamin Moore) 112 for base coat

Water glazes
- Glaze No. 1: eight parts Alizarin Crimson to four parts Burnt Umber to one part Mars Black
- Glaze No. 2: two parts Burnt Umber to one part Mars Black

Oil glaze: two parts Cassel Earth to one part Alizarin Crimson

Varnish and brush

Brushes for primers and base coat

Two No. 2 oval sash brushes for glaze application

¾" round pointed housepainters' brush

Worn or shredded sea sponge

Small, medium and large spalters

Badger blender

Bristle blender

Veinette or similar brush and comb

Tapes: painters', drafting and ⅛" automotive

Drawing tools: straightedge, ruler and pencil

Sandpaper

Whiting

Fine-grade synthetic scrubbing pad

Paint thinner for cleanup

Cotton swab (optional)

1 | Prime and base coat the chest with the same B.M. 112 as for the sample board. Sand lightly between coats and after the final base coat.

2 | Remove the drawers from the chest and tape them together so they form a single stacked unit. This will allow you to paint the crotch figure on all of them at once. Apply ¾" painters' tape to create a border for each drawer.

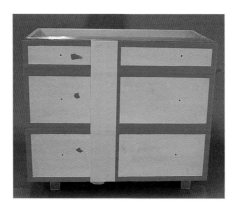

3 | Tape off half the front of the drawer stack with the ¾" tape, and back it up with 2" tape for extra protection. You are ready to paint the first piece of your mahogany crotch book-match.

4 | Apply the water glaze of eight parts Alizarin Crimson, four parts Cassel Earth, one part Mars Black. Use a medium spalter to lay out the glaze.

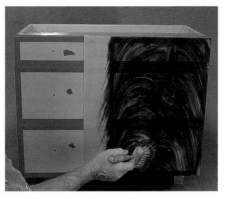

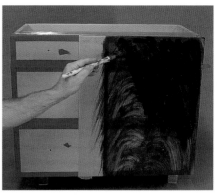

5 | Disregard the taped borders between the drawers, and using the round pointed housepainters' brush with the water glaze of two parts Burnt Umber to one part Mars Black, draw in the dark central figure.

6 | Repeating the steps shown in the mahogany crotch sample board, draw in the grain lines and soften them with the appropriate tools. Remember to soften out from the center as you finish off the central figure.

7 | When the water glaze is dry, apply the oil glaze of two parts Cassel Earth to one part Alizarin Crimson.

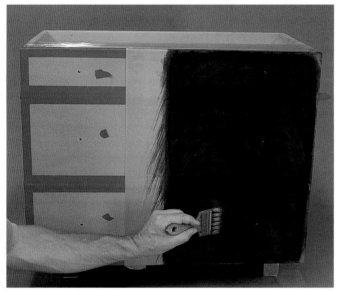

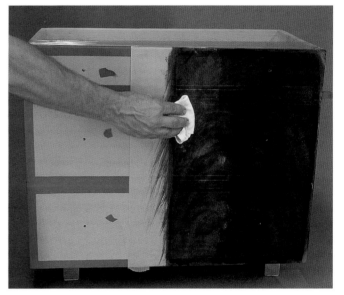

8 | Follow the procedures from the sample board to lay out, texture and soften the oil glaze to create additional grain lines and moirés.

9 | Allow the oil glaze to dry, then dust it lightly with whiting. This will reduce the possibility that tape applied over it will lift the glaze. Be sure the glaze is dry to the touch or the whiting will stick to it, creating a gritty finish. Brush off any extra whiting; you just want a light coating to prevent the tape from adhering permanently with the oil glaze. Then remove the tape from the center line.

10 | Apply drafting tape to the finished side of the drawer stack, then begin the graining on the second half of the book-match. Make the figure and grain lines as close as possible to a mirror image of the first side. It may take some extra effort to get it right. But don't panic if it doesn't look right. Just wipe off the water glaze and try again.

11 | Add the oil overglaze as you did on the first half to complete the book-match.

12 | Remove the tapes to reveal the finished book-matched panel on the stacked drawer fronts. When the glaze is dry, a coat of varnish will help protect the surface while you carry out the remaining steps.

13 | Remove the ¾" tape to reveal the unfinished borders on each drawer.

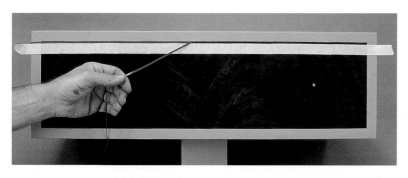

14 | This series of operations will allow you to make an inlay line between the crotch and the border in a different way. First, lay down a piece of ⅛" tape on the edge of the painted finish. This tape will only be used to temporarily establish the width of the inlay line. Then lay down the ¾" drafting tape on the painted finish, right next to the ⅛" tape. Remove the thin tape to reveal a ⅛" line of the finished area.

15 | Complete this process all the way around the drawer, exposing a ⅛" border. When you finish the border, the overlap of the two layers of finish will give the impression of a black line.

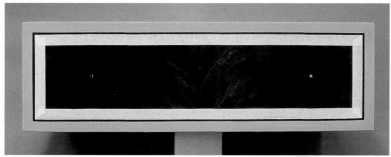

16 | Tape off mitered corners on two sides of the drawers, and deglaze the exposed finish with whiting and a light rub from a fine abrasive pad.

17 | Apply water glaze No. 1 (eight parts Alizarin Crimson, four parts Cassel Earth and one part Mars Black) to the border.

18 | Using a swab or a glaze brush, add streaks of the No. 2 water glaze (Burnt Umber and Mars Black) every few inches at right angles to the edge of the drawer.

19 | Create the grain by dragging a folded tissue through the two glaze colors. You will be developing a border effect known as cross banding. If you like, you can soften the effect by brushing in the direction of the cross banding with a small spalter or blending brush. Let dry.

20 | Apply the oil overglaze of two parts Cassel Earth to one part Alizarin Crimson, and soften with a small spalter in the direction of the cross banding. Let dry thoroughly.

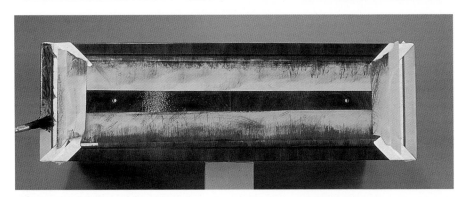

21 | Change the tapes so you can paint the other two sections of the cross banding using the same steps. Don't forget to finish the ends of the drawers. Let dry.

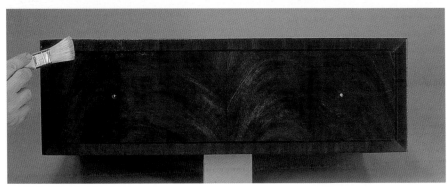

22 | Remove the tapes to reveal the completed book-match, cross banding and inlay combination. Give each drawer a coat of varnish to seal the finish.

23 | Finish the top of the case with a book-match crotch, as well. Make sure you tape the border with the ¾" painters' tape as you did on the drawers. The top with the first half already complete is shown. For variety, apply the crotch in opposite directions here rather than side by side as you did on the front.

24 | Once again, draw a mirror image of the first piece of veneer. Some difference is to be expected, but make sure the central figure has the correct tilt and similar shape. Complete the steps to make the crotch section and let dry.

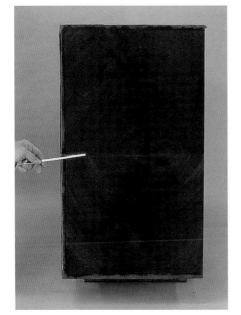

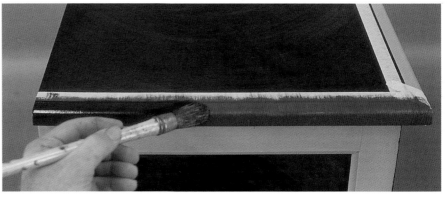

26 | Complete the top by finishing the borders with the same cross-banding technique you employed for the drawers.

25 | Remove the tape that separates the two halves, but leave the tape on the borders, and varnish the entire area. Let dry.

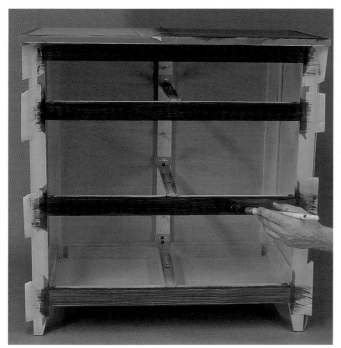

27 Tape off the stiles on the front of the chest, and paint the rails using the same three glazes you used on the crotch sections. Brush on the first water glaze, then lay in streaks of the darker water glaze and draw a damp sea sponge through the two glazes to develop the straight-grain mahogany. When the water glaze dries, apply the oil glaze and lay it out with a small spalter, then add some moirés.

28 After the rails dry, tape them off and do the stiles. For variation, substitute the medium spalter for the sea sponge to create the grain in the water glaze. Then overglaze these areas with the oil glaze.

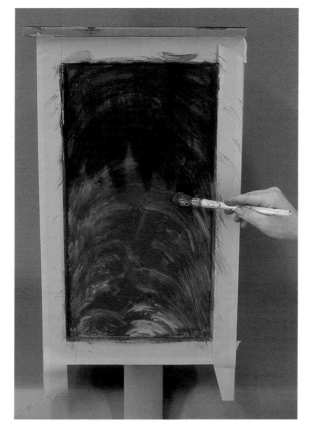

29 Tape off the end panels and, following the previously outlined procedures, develop a single crotch figure each. Once again, give the central plume a little tilt for a more dynamic quality.

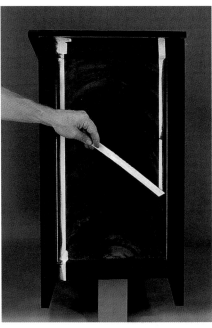

30 | When you have completed the end panel and it has dried, do the rails and stiles just as you did on the front of the chest.

31 | Use the spalter turned sideways to create the grain for the raised section of the rails and stiles.

32 | As with all other finished areas that you have taped over, slowly and carefully remove the tape from the central panel as soon as possible.

33 | Give the whole chest at least two coats of varnish, then let dry and reattach the knobs and replace the drawers.

country-grained jelly cabinet

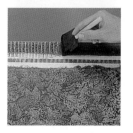

This type of cupboard, traditionally used in country kitchens for storing canned goods and kitchen implements, is a good choice for this folk-type of graining. The terms *country graining*, *vinegar painting* and *putty painting* all refer to the same type of decorative finishing. While the glazes you use are formulated just like the water glazes demonstrated elsewhere in this book, the results are more of an approximation of a "woody" look, rather than an attempt to simulate grain patterns of particular woods. This freedom of technique, commonly used by American craftsmen in the early 1800s, often resulted in wild color and pattern variation. Furniture that exhibits this exuberant type of finish is highly prized by collectors of 19th-century American antiques. If you are interested in learning more about this technique, please see my book *Decorative Furniture Finishes with Vinegar Paint* (North Light Books, 1999).

MATERIALS LIST

Primer

Palette and/or containers for glazes

French Yellow Ochre or similar color oil or latex/acrylic enamel for base coat

Vinegar glazes
• Burnt Umber
• Burnt Sienna
• Prussian Blue

Three No. 2 oval sash brushes for glaze application

Brushes for primer and base coat

Vinyl glazing compound or putty

2" foam brush

Feather

Varnish and brush

Sandpaper

Drawing tools: straightedge, ruler, pencil and drafting compass

Tapes: painters', drafting and 1/8" automotive

Paint thinner for cleanup

1 | The clean lines of this cupboard provide the opportunity to use a variety of colors and patterns to create a lively folk treatment. The piece here has been primed, and base painted with Muralo Ultra brand acrylic enamel. This paint works about as well as oil paint when it comes to providing a base for vinegar painting, but it has the added convenience of being a latex. This color, which Muralo calls Pigskin, closely approximates the French Yellow Ochre commonly used in the 1800s.

2 | Remove the door, and tape around the panels, then apply Burnt Umber vinegar glaze to one of the panels.

3 | Immediately stipple the area with the glaze brush, then touch in spots of Prussian Blue glaze. Stipple again to soften and redistribute the blue spots.

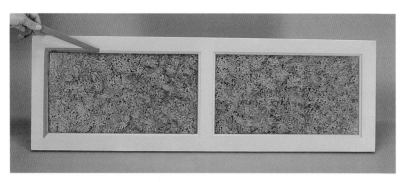

4 | Varnish each panel after it dries, then remove the tape from around them.

5 | Use drafting tape to mask off the panels.

6 | Use a straightedge to draw a pencil line around the rails and stiles, and tape along these lines with the ⅛" automotive masking tape. This tape will preserve a line of the base color in the final finish.

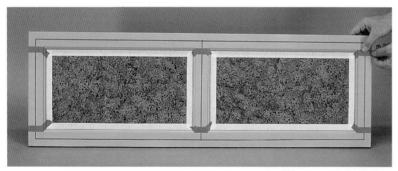

7 | Tape off the rails from the stiles.

8 | Apply Burnt Umber glaze to the whole stile, and immediately press into the wet glaze with a finger-shaped piece of the glazing compound. Finish the whole length of the stile before the glaze dries. If the glaze sets up before you finish, rewet the whole area and try again, working more quickly.

9 | Complete both stiles in this fashion, making sure to texture the edges as you go. Varnish them when they dry.

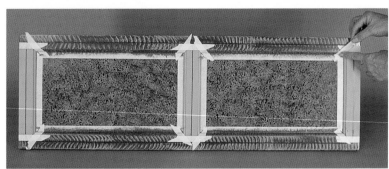

10 | After the varnish dries, remove the painters' tape from the rails and apply drafting tape to the stiles.

11 | Glaze and texture the rails as you did the stiles, and varnish them.

12 | Remove all the drafting tape and then the ⅛" tape. If any paint has run under the ⅛" tape, use a cotton swab dipped in vinegar medium to wipe it up.

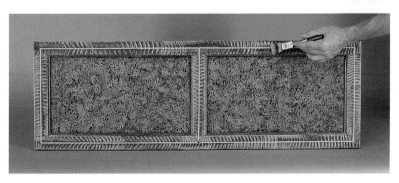

13 | Give the entire door at least two additional coats of varnish to protect the finish.

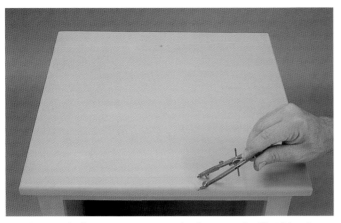

14 | Use a drafting compass or straightedge to mark off a ¾" border on the top of the cupboard. Notice there is no border on the back edge of the top.

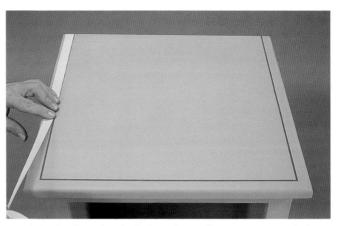

15 | Apply ⅛" tape beside the line, then wider tape to protect the border. Make sure the wide tape overlaps the thin tape.

16 | Apply the Burnt Umber and Prussian Blue stippled finish just as you did on the door panels. Then varnish when dry.

17 | Change the wide tape to protect the center panel, then grain the borders with the Burnt Sienna vinegar paint and glazing compound using the same procedures as you did on the door rails and styles. I usually do the two sides and then finish off the front to complete the border.

18 | After you have grained and varnished the entire border, remove the wide and narrow tape, and apply at least two more coats of varnish to complete and protect the finish.

19 | Grain the three sides of the base by brushing on the Burnt Sienna vinegar paint and texturing it with a feather. Varnish when dry. This will give a textural variation to the piece but retain the color continuity from the door frame and top border.

20 | Turn the piece on its side and measure and draw a central panel with a border similar to the way the door is constructed. Leave an area around the border that corresponds to the part of the case that shows around the door. You may eliminate the central rail as I have done or include it if you wish. Mask off the side so you can grain the border first. Mark the panel with small pieces of tape so it will be clear where not to paint. This may appear overly cautious, but mistakes of this sort can and do happen!

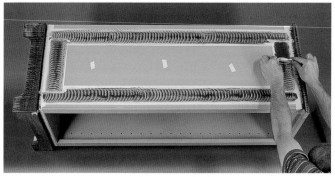

21 | Grain the border first this time because, unlike with the top and door, you will need to paint on both sides. Although I grained the stiles first and then the rails, you may reverse the order if you wish.

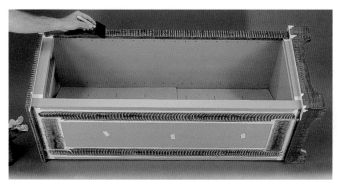

22 | While the side is drying, turn the case on its back and grain the parts of the case that show around the door. Apply the Burnt Umber glaze with spots of Prussian Blue, creating a linear grain pattern by pressing the tip of a sponge brush rapidly into the paint as you move along the surface. Do the two front stiles, varnish, then change the tapes and complete the rails.

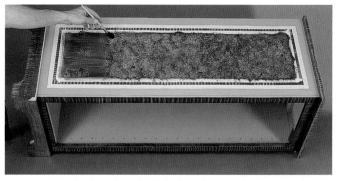

23 | Now go back to the side, and when the varnish on the border is dry, change the tape to cover it and stipple the central panel with the Burnt Umber, Prussian Blue combination you used on the other panels. Varnish when dry.

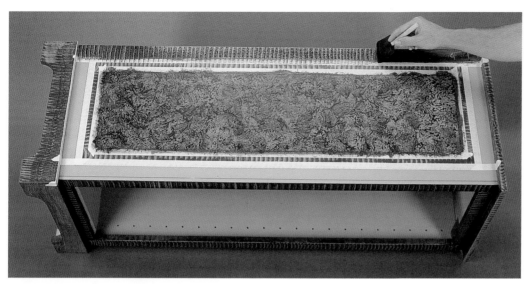

24 | Complete the sides by graining and varnishing the outer portions just as you did on the front of the case.

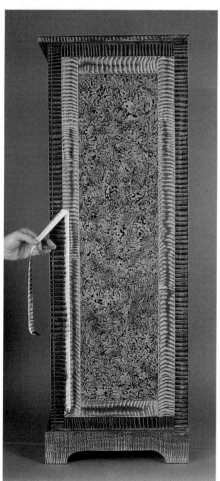

25 | Remove the tapes from the side of the case to reveal the completed design.

26 | With both sides finished, replace the door and hardware to complete the project.

weathered pine blanket chest

A large box like this provides storage space and can be used as a low table. If you plan to use it as a table, grain all four sides. For the top, front and back, do two versions of the sample board, creating a chevron design. Since this wood treatment is intended to look as though it has been affected by unusual growing or storage conditions, feel free to experiment with the glaze colors once you have mastered the manipulation. Simple black linear detail adds a touch of sophistication to this rustic treatment.

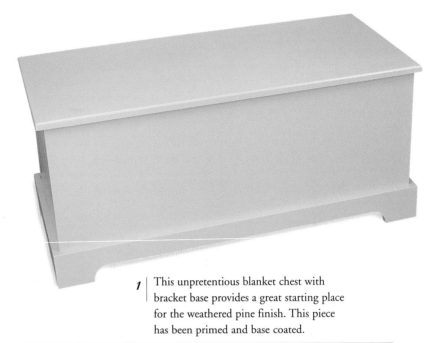

1 This unpretentious blanket chest with bracket base provides a great starting place for the weathered pine finish. This piece has been primed and base coated.

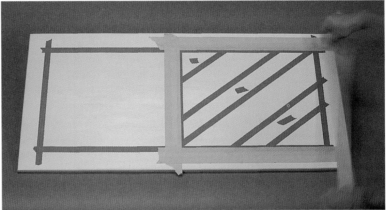

2 Beginning with the lid removed from the chest, draw and tape off a design similar to the weathered pine sample board. Use two diagonal panels to create a chevron pattern with the point toward the front of the chest. Small pieces of tape placed on alternate panels indicate those to be masked off and finished later.

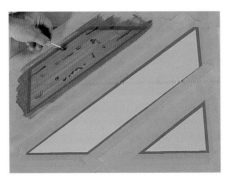

3 In one of the exposed areas, brush on the oil glaze of three parts Raw Sienna to one part Burnt Umber, then with cotton swabs touch in the extra "weathering" colors of Burnt Umber, Burnt Sienna, Cassel Earth and Mars Black.

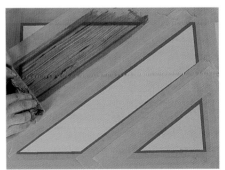

4 Lightly blend the colors with a small spalter, then grain with a twisting motion of the burlap. Complete the other three diagonal sections and let dry overnight.

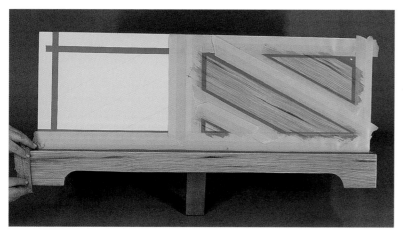

5 | While these sections are drying, draw and tape a similar design on the chest front and back (if desired). The chevron should point up. Tape off the design, and grain the alternate panels. Begin to grain the base at this time.

6 | Continue to work on the ends of the chest with a single angular panel and frame just like the design of the sample board.

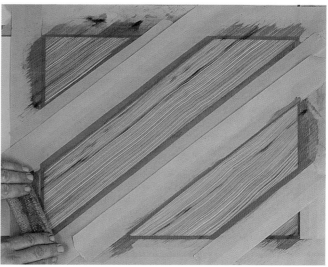

7 | As the front, back and end panels are drying, move back to the top. Dust the dry oil glaze with whiting, then apply the water overglaze of two parts Raw Sienna to one part Burnt Umber. Lay out the glaze with a spalter, then texture with the folded cheesecloth. It will dry quickly, so you can varnish these areas almost immediately. Let the varnish dry overnight.

8 | When the varnish is dry, carefully remove the tape and mask off the finished areas. Then repeat the graining technique on the new sections. Although I used the blue painters' tape for this operation, I strongly suggest you use drafting tape if your finish has had less than three days to cure. Drafting tape is less likely to lift the finish when you remove it.

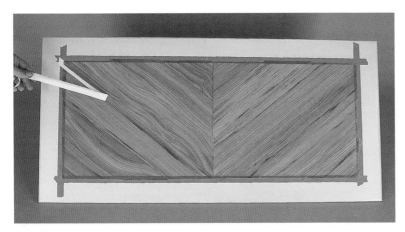

9 | After you complete one side of the chevron, move to the other panel and continue until the whole central area is grained and varnished.

10 | Mask off the central panels, and grain the frame with the same technique. Do the two end sections at the same time, then the top and bottom. Remember to continue graining over the end of an exposed board.

11 | When the individual frame sections are dry, overglaze them with a water glaze of two parts Raw Sienna, one part Burnt Umber and one part Kremer Translucent Red. Let dry and varnish.

12 | While you are waiting for the glazes and varnish to dry on the top, continue working with the front, back and sides. As you complete the top, you should be nearly finished graining the other parts also.

13 | To add a touch of sophistication after you have finished all the graining, add black rectangular borders with the lining tool to emphasize the individual diagonal panels.

problems working with burlap?

It is very difficult to get the folded burlap graining tool into inside corners, such as where the vertical frame sections on the chest meet the bracket base. This can give rise to unconvincing work, as you will either be unable to texture the glaze (if you start your stroke there) or you will leave a deposit of extra glaze (if that is where you complete the stroke). Solve this problem by wrapping the burlap over a piece of cardboard, then placing this "hard" tool into the corner. Complete the graining stroke with the same motion you would use with the folded burlap. Since the tool is now hard, you won't have to exert as much pressure to create the grain lines in the glaze.

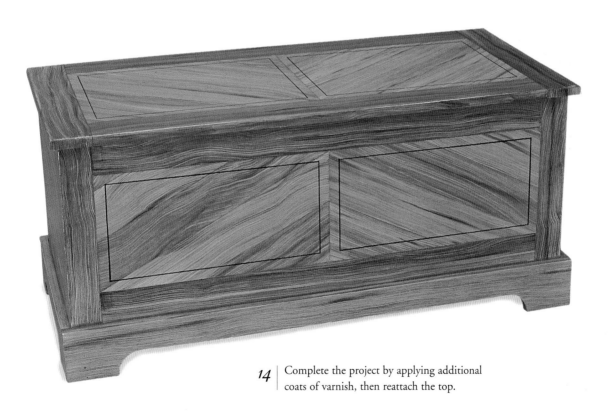

14 | Complete the project by applying additional coats of varnish, then reattach the top.

bird's-eye corner unit

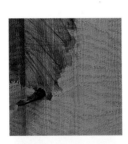

This corner cabinet, designed as an entertainment center to hold a T.V., stereo or other media, is a good project for the more ambitious, confident, grain painter. Graining will not only allow you to vary the appearance of the piece according to your design needs but will also allow you to conceal glued-up door panels and any minor surface blemishes. Keep in mind that you will need to consider how the inside will look when the doors are open during use.

MATERIALS LIST

Primer

Palette and/or containers for glazes

B.M. (Benjamin Moore) 180 for base coat

Brushes for primer and base coat

Brown or other color oil paint for interior of cabinet

Yellow Ochre or similar oil paint for door frame

Water glazes
• Glaze No. 1: one part Cassel Brown and one part Raw Sienna
• Glaze No. 2: one part Burnt Umber to one part Mars Black for the door frames

Oil glaze: one part Cassel Brown to one part Raw Sienna

Varnish and brush

Two No. 2 oval sash brushes for glaze application

Small and medium spalters

Badger blender

No. 8 fan brush or veinette and comb

Oil-blending brush

Small cellulose sponge to create straight grain

Plastic wrap

Fine-grade synthetic scrubbing pad (optional)

Whiting

Sandpaper

Newspaper to protect finished surfaces

Paint thinner for cleanup

Drafting or painters' tape

Spray shellac (optional)

Sponge for deglazing (optional)

1 | While this is a large piece, the surfaces are mostly flat. The mouldings and door frames will require added attention due to their dimensional nature.

2 | Begin by priming and sanding the doors. Then paint the panels with low-luster alkyd B.M. 180. Prepare both sides of the doors now to cut the risk of getting base paint on the finished sides later on.

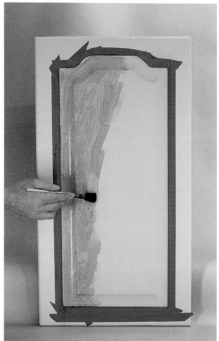

3 | Using drafting or painters' tape, mask off the stiles and rails.

4 | With a No. 2 sash brush, apply a thin coat of the water glaze of Cassel Brown and Raw Sienna. The more Raw Sienna you use in the mixture and the thinner you apply it, the more subtle the pattern will be.

5 | Working quickly, use a medium spalter to lay out the glaze, stroking across the panel first and finishing up lengthwise. If the glaze dries before you can finish this process, you must apply a wetter coat and start over.

6 | Wipe the spalter clean with a cloth and lay in the moirés, working from top to bottom. After each pass down the panel, wipe the spalter with the cloth again. A wavy mottler may also be used for this step.

7 | As soon as you finish the moirés, soften horizontally with the badger blender. Only the lightest touch is necessary.

8 | While the surface is still damp, with your moistened fingertip touch in the "eyes" in groups of twos and threes, with a few singles.

9 | Soften with the badger blender in one direction diagonally. Let dry.

10 | You have the option at this point to seal the first glaze. Doing so will prevent you from having to redo it if you have a problem with the next glaze, which is also water based. To seal this first glaze, apply a thin coat of spray shellac to the surface and let it dry to the touch, about 30 minutes. If you feel confident that you can complete the next glaze without mishap, you may delete this step and the next and go right to the second glaze application.

11 | After the shellac dries, deglaze it with a fine-grade scrubbing pad. A light rub is all that is needed, but you must be sure to cover the entire panel. If the next glaze beads up on the surface, you will have to repeat the deglazing process.

12 | For the second glaze application, use a veinette or fan brush with the bristles separated. Lay in the straight grain with the same glaze used for the first layer. Make sure the lines do not cross each other, and try to keep the spacing consistent. You will need to reload the veinette after each pass. Slight trembling of the hand as you make these lines will add interest.

13 | After the lines dry, brush on the oil glaze consisting of Cassel Brown and Raw Sienna artists' oil color. This glaze should be only slightly darker than the water glaze used for the first two layers.

14 | Lay out the glaze with a small spalter, as always finishing in the long direction of the panel.

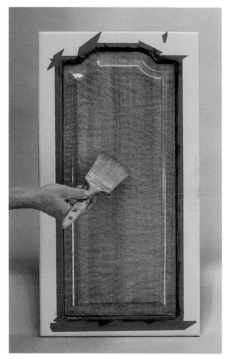

16 | Working in the long direction of the panel only, soften this oil glaze with a bristle blender, leaving only subtle tone variations. This completes the panel treatment. Doing a pair of doors at the same time will help maintain continuity of color and pattern. For added protection, varnish the panel after the oil glaze is thoroughly dry. This may take a day or two, depending on how you have formulated your glaze and the drying conditions.

15 | With a piece of pleated plastic food wrap, press into the wet glaze to add a subtle series of moirés.

17 | After the panel is varnished and dry, remove the tape from the rails and stiles, and mask over the panel. Cover the entire panel to prevent any concern about drips or splatters.

18 | Paint the rails and stiles with Yellow Ochre or a similar color oil paint.

19 | Tape off the stiles and deglaze the rails with whiting and a sponge or a fine scrubbing pad.

20 | Before beginning this step, refer to the section in the chapter "Woodgraining Techniques" on "pulling" straight grain. Brush on a heavy wet coat of a water glaze of equal parts Burnt Umber and Mars Black.

21 | Quickly stipple the inside edge of the rail with the same No. 2 sash brush used to apply the paint. This is necessary because it is nearly impossible to grain this area with the sponge, as you will the front and outside edge of the door.

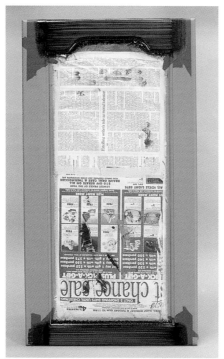

22 | Hold the small piece of dampened synthetic sponge slightly on edge and pull it straight through the wet glaze. Be sure to start on the tape, and in one motion, continue through the wet glaze until the sponge is on the tape at the end. If the results are not satisfactory, you may rewet the glaze and try again.

23 | Grain the other rail and varnish them both.

24 | When the varnish dries, tape the rails and grain the stiles in the same fashion.

25 | When using the sponge, you may get better results by holding it with two hands to equalize the pressure and keep the lines straight. Varnish the stiles when the glaze dries.

26 | Remove all the masking and give the entire door two coats of varnish to complete this part of the project. Repeat the process on the door backs if desired.

27 | To continue, prime and paint the interior with an appropriate color (I chose a deep brown). Prime and base coat the exterior of the piece with the same base color as the door panels.

28 | Tape off the front panels and the top and bottom mouldings, and grain the sides with the same technique used on the door panels. For tonal variety, use a slightly heavier application of the first glaze. As this is a larger surface, you will need to work quickly to finish the moirés before the glaze sets up.

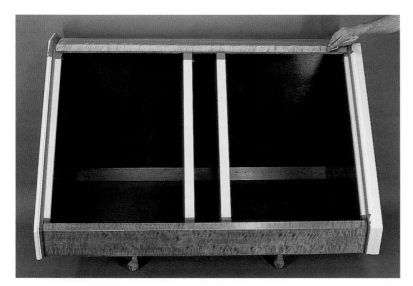

29 For both sides of the carcass, complete all the steps done on the door panels. If you find it difficult to work vertically, lay the piece down and work horizontally. This may give you better control of the media.

31 Finish the front panels with the same technique and color. Be sure to finish the top lip of these panels as they will show when the doors are open.

30 When the sides are finished, remove the tape from the front panels and mask the finished areas as well as the top and bottom mouldings.

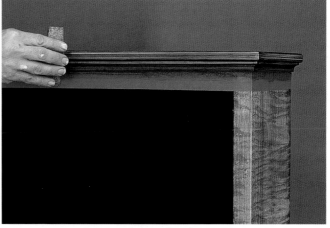

32 Finish the top and bottom mouldings with the same pattern and colors you used on the stiles and rails of the doors. Add two or more coats of varnish to complete the project.

GALLERY

This French provincial-style chest, with all its curves, would be difficult to grain convincingly as a specific wood, but benefits beautifully from a vinegar paint treatment.

You can use the oak graining technique to give a small lamp table some special character.

Zebrawood graining used to suggest marquetry creates a lively pattern for this slender hall table.

By alternating elm and amboyna burl effects, you can create interesting geometric patterns, as I did for this cocktail table (left and below). For variety, I finished the base in walnut.

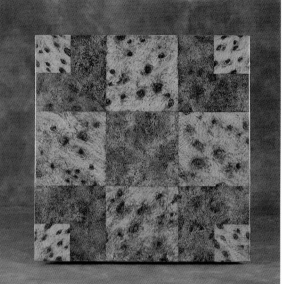

Macassar ebony graining adds an exotic air to this tall lingerie chest.

This small chair, with its many corners and surfaces, is well-suited to the decorative effects of vinegar painting.

TROUBLESHOOTING

PROBLEM: *Base paints or primers have a rough appearance.*

CAUSE: The paint dried before the brush marks flowed out, or runs and curtains have formed.

SOLUTIONS: (1) Thin paint with appropriate solvent so it will flow out; (2) apply less paint to avoid runs; (3) make sure to lay out paint in the direction of the grain of the wood; (4) use better quality brush and/or paint; (5) sand with medium-grit paper between each and every coat.

PROBLEM: *Water glaze beads up on surface.*

CAUSE: Base-paint surface is too slick or oily.

SOLUTION: Deglaze surface with whiting or abrasive pad prior to glaze application.

PROBLEM: *Glaze dries before appropriate manipulation can be performed.*

CAUSES: (1) Oil glaze has too much solvent; (2) Water glaze has too much pigment; (3) Temperature in studio is too high; (4) Manipulation is too slow.

SOLUTIONS: (1) Reformulate oil glaze to stay wet longer by adding more linseed oil or replacing some of the paint thinner (up to 10 percent) with kerosene; (2) add more water or vinegar to water glaze; (3) lower temperature in work area if possible; (4) practice manipulation so it can be accomplished more quickly; or (4) have an assistant apply glaze so that you can concentrate on manipulation.

PROBLEM: *Underlying glaze is lifted or moved when new glaze or varnish is applied.*

CAUSE: Oil glazes must thoroughly dry before another solvent-based product is applied, or the solvent in the new layer may dissolve the underglaze; water glazes can be disturbed by vigorous rubbing or careless application of a second water glaze.

SOLUTIONS: (1) Allow oil underglazes to completely dry (if linseed oil medium is used, this will take overnight); (2) use alkyd glaze medium with oil glazes (they will dry more quickly); (3) when dry, seal either oil or water glazes with a coat of spray shellac, which will prevent a new glaze or friction from disturbing them.

PROBLEM: *The final result is murky or too dark.*

CAUSE: Too much pigment has obscured the base paint or underglaze.

SOLUTION: Adjust the glaze by reducing the proportion of paint to medium. This will result in greater transparency.

PROBLEM: *Glaze leaks under edge of tape.*

CAUSE: Edge of tape is not tight to surface.

SOLUTION: Burnish edge of tape with fingernail or other smooth object before applying glaze.

PROBLEM: *Tape pulls up paint or glaze.*

CAUSES: (1) Paint or glaze has not thoroughly dried before tape was applied; (2) the tape was too sticky; (3) tape was left on too long.

SOLUTIONS: (1) Allow paint or glaze to thoroughly dry before applying tape; (2) avoid conventional masking tape; (3) if tape must be left on for more than a day, use drafting tape, as it does not degrade as fast as painters' tape.

PROBLEM: *When sanding between coats of final finish, some of the glaze is sanded away.*

CAUSE: Sanding was too vigorous for the amount of varnish on the surface.

SOLUTIONS: (1) Begin sanding the final finish only after two coats of varnish have been applied; (2) use finer sandpaper so less material is sanded away; (3) sand lightly before applying a new coat of varnish.

SOURCES FOR TOOLS AND MATERIALS

A good paint store should carry a wide range of painting supplies as well as one or more brands of nationally recognized paints. Housepainters' glazes, sanding papers, painters' tape, brushes, varnishes, shellac and other standard finishing materials should be in regular stock. The owner, manager or staff should be able to help you with particular finishing and painting problems. While the prices may be slightly higher than those of the large home centers, the expertise and personal attention will more than make up the difference.

AUTOMOTIVE PAINT STORES

Look in the yellow pages under "Automobile, body and paint supplies" to find sources for ⅛" automotive masking tape, or ask at your local body shop. They may even agree to sell you some from their stock. Remember, this tape is blue like the painters' tape, but it has a plastic base as opposed to a paper one.

BILL RUSSELL STUDIO
1215 Frankford Ave.
Philadelphia, PA 19125
215-203-0068
www.billrussellstudio.com
rusgal@worldnet.att.net

Offers decorative painting services and workshops in various decorative painting techniques as well as a decorative painting kit for country graining. Call, write or e-mail to be added to our mailing list or for more information.

CONSTANTINE'S WOODWORKING SUPPLY
2050 Eastchester Rd.
Bronx, NY 10461
800-223-8087
www.constantines.com

Tools, hardware and finishing supplies for woodworkers and furniture restoration. Carries a wide variety of veneers that allows you to see what a specific wood looks like.

DANIEL SMITH ART SUPPLY
4150 First Ave., S.
P.O. Box 84268
Seattle, WA 98124-5568
800-426-6740
www.danielsmith.com

GARRETT WADE
161 Avenue of the Americas
New York, NY 10013
800-221-2942
www.garrettwade.com

High-quality woodworking and finishing supplies.

KREMER PIGMENTS, INC.
228 Elizabeth St.
New York, NY 10012
800-995-5501
www.kremer-pigmente.de/englisch/homee.htm

The ultimate pigment source. Thirteen types of black! Also a good source for unusual painting supplies, including brushes. The catalog may be a bit daunting for beginners, but the representatives are very helpful.

LONDON GROVE INDUSTRIES, INC.
431 W. Baltimore Pike
West Grove, PA 19390
610-869-0700
www.londongrove.com

Manufacturer of ready-to-finish maple furniture.

MOHAWK FINISHING PRODUCTS, INC.
4715 State Highway 30
Amsterdam, NY 12010
(800) 545-0047
www.mohawk-finishing.com

Supplies for the professional finisher: If it is used in wood finishing, this company probably carries it.

MURALO PAINT CORP. AND ELDER JENKS BRUSHES
148 E. Fifth St.
Bayonne, NJ 07002
800-631-3440
www.muralocompany.com

Manufacturers of the Ultra line of water-based house paint that performs similarly to oil paint. Also makes high-quality No. 2 natural bristle oval sash brushes. A representative should be able to help you find a source in your area.

PEARL PAINTS NORTH AMERICA, INC.
15600 S. Lathrop
Harvey, IL 60426
708-596-2300
www.pearlpaints.com

Other locations around the United States. Excellent range of artists' and craft supplies, including decorative painting materials.

3M CORPORATION
3M Center
St. Paul, MN 55144-1000
800-364-3577 (Helpline)
www.3M.com

Manufacturers of painters' tapes and specialty sandpapers.

WILLIAM ZINSSER & CO., INC.
173 Belmont Dr.
Somerset, NJ 08875
732-469-4367
www.zinsser.com

Manufacturer of specialty paints and primers.

WOODWORKER'S SUPPLY
1108 N. Glenn Rd.
Casper, WY 82601
800-645-9292

Catalog company. Carries a wide variety of finishing supplies, including Behlen's Wool Lube, and 3M sandpaper for sanding latex and acrylic paints.

INDEX